The
420
Gourmet

The 420 Gourmet

The Elevated Art of Cannabis Cuisine

JeffThe420Chef

Recipe Photography by Leela Cyd

HARPER WAVE

An Imprint of HarperCollinsPublishers

This book contains advice and information relating to health care.
It is not intended to replace medical advice and should be used to supplement rather than
replace regular care by your doctor. It is recommended that you seek your physician's
advice before embarking on any medical program or treatment. All efforts have
been made to ensure the accuracy of the information contained in this book as of the date
of publication. The publisher and the author disclaim liability for any medical outcomes
that may occur as a result of applying the methods suggested in this book.

HarperCollins books may be purchased for educational, business, or sales
promotional use. For information, please e-mail the Special Markets Department at
SPsales@harpercollins.com.

FIRST EDITION

Designed by Laura Palese

Recipe photography by Leela Cyd

Cannabis photography by Michael Burnham

Library of Congress Cataloging-in-Publication Data

JeffThe420Chef.
The 420 gourmet : the elevated art of cannabis cuisine / JeffThe420Chef; photography
by Leela Cyd.—First edition.
Includes bibliographical references and index.
pages   cm
ISBN 978-0-06-244505-6
1. LCSH: Cooking (Marijuana). 2. Marijuana—Therapeutic use. 3. Cookbooks.
TX819.M25 J442016
394.1′4—dc23
2016004092
16 17 18 19 20   OV/QUAD   10 9 8 7 6 5 4 3 2 1

THIS BOOK IS DEDICATED TO each medical marijuana patient now able to benefit from the legalization of medical cannabis, to the state lawmakers who are changing the laws to allow people to medicate with this incredible herb, and to all those who helped pave the path that we are now on with blood, sweat, and prison time.

Also to my three incredible sons, Matt, Jared, and Zach, who have encouraged and supported me from the moment I dreamed up this whacky idea of becoming a cannabis chef. And to my parents, who were gracious enough to take me back in as a "starving author" in L.A. after I let go of everything in New York to bring JeffThe420Chef to life. I could not have done any of this without you all by my side.

This is *not* your
mother's cookbook!

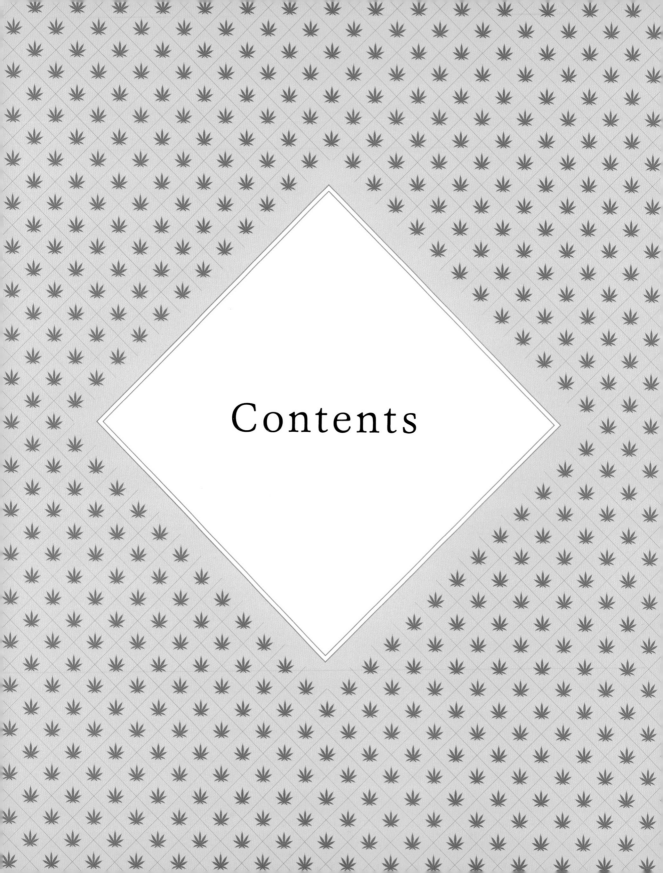

Contents

Preface

FROM AS EARLY as I can remember, I have loved cooking and baking. When I was six (and just learning to read), my favorite birthday present was a kids' cookbook. I learned how to make all the basics, like cinnamon toast and English muffin pizza. And I also learned that the quickest way to make people feel good is to cook something delicious and share it with them. Like any precocious little boy, I got into my share of trouble. All I had to do to make things better was head to the kitchen and make something yummy to share, and all was forgotten.

While I have always been interested in food and cooking, it wasn't until 2012 that I began to incorporate cannabis into my recipes. At the time, a friend's mother was being treated for cancer, and she had a medical marijuana prescription to help with her pain and nausea. Around the same time, I stumbled upon an interview with Dr. Raphael Mechoulam—an Israeli organic chemist and professor of medicinal chemistry at the Hebrew University of Jerusalem in Israel—who has been at the forefront of cannabis research for many decades. Through this interview, I found out about the medicinal compound in cannabis called cannabidiol (CBD) that helps with numerous health issues, especially when combined with a low dose of tetrahydrocannabinol (THC).

On the basis of that knowledge, I decided to start making edibles for my friend's mother that were different from the average edibles that were being sold. At that time, you'd buy an edible in a dispensary and have no clue what you were getting (and you still don't always know). Was it a sativa or an indica strain? What was the percentage of THC? Did it contain the medicinal compound CBD? No one really knew. Dispensaries at that point were generally selling edibles that were heavy on the THC, which didn't really help my friend's mother at all; they just made her feel loopy, which is not what she wanted. Instead, she needed edibles made from strains with more CBD, in addition to the THC—and that's what I was able to provide.

A close friend was suffering from fibromyalgia and debilitating PMS that involved joint pain and headaches around the same time. She complained that although she had a medical marijuana recommendation, she didn't smoke, and the edibles she bought didn't help her either—they just got her high. The more I researched, the more I learned about certain strains, like Cannatonic and Harlequin, that could really help with these and other physical ailments. I figured if I could learn how to properly dose my edibles with the right CBD:THC ratio, I could help people feel even better. I decided to cook a few dishes with high-CBD strains in the hope that the benefits of cannabis would help ease her suffering— and it worked. I was starting to see, firsthand, the incredible medicinal power of cooking with cannabis.

Another friend suffering from chronic migraines and pain after major knee surgery asked me to make her a cake with a new strain of God's Blueberry, a high-CBD strain that she had gotten from a local dispensary. By then, I was cooking for several people with medical marijuana recommendations. She called me the next day shouting, "I have no pain! Please teach me how to do this on my own." I did, and I have been teaching people how to cook with cannabis ever since.

After these early forays, I became obsessed with learning more about cannabis and how it can actually help people suffering from a multitude of ailments. Like many people, I had already known about THC, the main psychoactive compound of cannabis. But I learned that CBD is the unsung hero of cannabis; this non-psychoactive ingredient is proved to be the powerful medicinal compound in the plant. And I learned about the entourage effect, which is the interaction of the many healing compounds within each cannabis strain that allows the plant to help individuals facing various medical challenges. I call it "medical manna."

The science of cannabis is fairly new, and it's an ongoing learning process, as new information appears nearly every week. Most of what I have learned is from the published works of cannabis scientists such as the aforementioned Dr. Raphael Mechoulam, the grandfather of medical cannabis research and winner of numerous awards for his discoveries. At the age of eighty-four, he continues to research the chemistry of cannabis and how the chemical compounds, known as cannabinoids, help alleviate pain, reduce inflammation, lower high blood pressure, strengthen bones, shrink tumors, prevent seizures, promote healing, alleviate many of the side effects of chemotherapy, and even kill cancer cells.

According to the American Cancer Society, several clinical studies have proved that cannabis is helpful in treating nausea and vomiting from cancer chemotherapy, and that it can help treat pain caused by damaged nerves and appetite. But more recently, scientists reported that THC and CBD (along with other cannabinoids) can slow the growth and/or cause the death of certain types of cancer cells in lab tests. While most of these studies were based on smoking cannabis, Dr. Mechoulam and other cannabis researchers report that edibles help the same way—they are just metabolized differently. The more I learned from the research, the more I realized that my desire to help others feel good had taken on a new level of meaning and impact when I began cooking with cannabis. My love of food and cooking could now help others feel good on an entirely different scale.

In the beginning, I prepared only cannabis-infused appetizers and dessert items. I focused on cooking and baking with strains that were high in CBD, and the edibles actually worked! Word quickly spread, which led to my cooking full meals of cannabis-infused foods. Most strains of cannabis that contain a high percentage of CBD also have a fair amount of THC in them, which causes strong psychoactive effects. Creating edibles and full meals that didn't impart a heavy dose of THC was tricky. This meant I had to focus on *low dosing*, which allows people to have a full cannabis-infused meal or a handful of delicious homemade cookies, rather than just a bite or two of a not-so-great-tasting commercial cookie.

With this expansion of options and variety, the issue of the taste came to the forefront. Some folks do like the cannabis taste in their edibles, but most others don't—especially when it's present in every course of a meal. Even if you enjoy the taste of cannabis, you probably don't want *everything* to taste as if it has cannabis in it. So creating great-tasting edibles, in which the cannabis taste was muted—or, better yet, nonexistent—became a passion of mine. It took me almost a year and a half to figure it out, but in 2014, I finally discovered how to create "light-tasting" and "virtually tasteless" edibles. Once I mastered low-dosed, great-tasting gourmet edibles, my 420 meals and infused edibles quickly gained popularity—and I became one of a select few private chefs to develop and cater custom gourmet cannabis experiences for medicinal and recreational users alike.

Now that I've figured out the main challenges of taste and dosing when it comes to cooking with cannabis, I am happy to share some of my secrets with you. So let's have some fun and make some edibles! If there is one thing I've learned over the last fifty-three years, it's that *the secret to happiness and fulfillment is making others feel good*. And what better way to do that than through great food—and cannabis!

· PART ·

1

Highlighting
Cannabis

Introduction

WELCOME TO *THE 420 GOURMET*! The book you are holding is a compilation of everything I have learned so far about cooking with cannabis, and I am thrilled to be able to share it with you. The goal of this cookbook is to inform recreational and medicinal cannabis users alike about how best to approach cooking and baking with this magical herb. The opening sections present an overview of cannabis, a look at some of the more popular strains and their effects, and important information on calculations and dosage. Please read this information carefully, as the key to a happy and successful edible experience relies on choosing the right strains and knowing how to properly calculate the levels of CBD and THC consumed.

Once you're ready to get started in the kitchen, I'll walk you through the infusion process so that you can infuse cannabis into butters and oils, creating the canna-butter and canna-oil that serve as the basis for all of my edibles. From there, I present more than 100 different cannabis-infused recipes, all of which were developed during my five years of cooking for others as JeffThe420Chef. These recipes will hopefully broaden your edible horizons far beyond the idea of pot brownies. From Canna-Coconut Lime Smoothies to Freaky Fish Tacos, from Krazy Kale & Hemp Seed Salad to Fantasy Focaccia, and from Buzzed Chickpea Curry to Canna-Apple Roses, there's something for everyone here—and for every meal.

In my work as JeffThe420Chef, I'm aiming to bring edibles to a tastier, more inclusive place, and to add legitimacy to the little-known benefits of cooking and baking with cannabis. With the proper approach and dosage, you can enjoy an entire meal of cannabis-infused foods, rather than just one or two bites of a traditional edible. My goal here is to make you comfortable cooking with cannabis so that you can unlock the mind and health benefits of marijuana in the most delicious way possible. Bon appétit!

UNDERSTANDING CANNABIS

BEFORE YOU START COOKING WITH CANNABIS, *it's essential to know and understand the ingredients with which you are working. Knowledge of the herb itself is a good place to start, along with details about the various strains and their effects. Having a handle on this information will allow you to have a safe, enjoyable edible experience.*

SATIVA	INDICA	HYBRID
Euphoric	Euphoric	A mixed bag of effects, depending on the "parents" of the strain. Hybrids will usually be either sativa- or indica-heavy. Check the database at leafly.com (more on this below) to see what a particular hybrid strain is known for.
Happy	Relaxed	
Talkative	Sleepy	
Giggly	Calm	
Philosophical	"Couch lock"	
"Head" high	"Body" high	

Cannabis Species: Sativa vs. Indica vs. Hybrids

There are two primary species or types of cannabis: sativa and indica. Each of these species is distinct in appearance and in the effects it imparts. One is generally known to make you perky (sativa), and one is generally known to make you more relaxed (indica). Crossbreeding of the two types is what produces hybrid strains, of which there are many (and each has its own unique characteristics). All cannabis strains are categorized according to their "personality traits" as either sativa, indica, or hybrid (and within the hybrid categorization there are sativa-heavy hybrids and indica-heavy hybrids).

Appearance-wise, sativa plants are tall with long thin leaves, and indica plants are short and bushy with broad leaves. Hybrids are usually dominant one way or the other and can impart a mix of effects. The chart above outlines the general psychoactive and physical effects of each species.

Strains

Within the three main classifications of cannabis—sativa, indica, and hybrid—there are many, many different strains available. You're likely wondering which strain of cannabis you should use when cooking or baking your edibles—and that's a tricky question. Leafly.com, the leading authority on cannabis, lists more than 1,500 various strains of cannabis, mostly hybrids, and each has its own unique characteristics and imparts its own effects. And to make it even more challenging, the database of strains is constantly growing. This is why it's so important to first decide on the experience you want from your edibles, and then to choose a strain that has the characteristics for which you are looking. While leafly.com has an excellent search engine that allows you to research most strains and quickly get the information you need to make an informed choice, we'll also go through some basics here to get you started.

Cannabinoids

If we dig a little deeper, we get to the core of what creates the differences between cannabis strains: the balance of each plant's compounds. According to United Patients Groups, a leading resource for medical cannabis information, scientists have identified more than 483 compounds in cannabis. More than 80 of these compounds are found only in cannabis plants and are known as cannabinoids. When cannabis is consumed, cannabinoids bind to receptor sites throughout the brain and body. Different cannabinoids have different effects, depending on which receptors they bind to. While we do not know the medicinal effects of the vast majority of these compounds, we do know that THC and CBD, the two primary cannabinoids in cannabis, have been shown in scientific studies to engage receptor sites throughout the brain and immune system that trigger potent healing and painkilling effects.

Here is a further introduction to the properties of THC and CBD, the two main compounds found in cannabis:

THC (tetrahydrocannabinol) is the psychoactive compound in the cannabis plant that gets you "high," but it also has therapeutic elements. So in addition to being the chemical responsible for feelings of euphoria and other mind-altering effects, it is also the part of the plant that helps alleviate nausea and boost appetite. On top of that, scientists have proved that it inhibits an enzyme implicated in the formation of beta-amyloid plaque, the hallmark of Alzheimer's-related dementia. Many medical patients who seek the uplifting and euphoric effects of cannabis in addition to medicinal effects, along with recreational users who enjoy the heady effects of the plant, will look for higher percentages of THC in the bud they consume. The higher the percentage of THC, the more psychoactively potent the strain. In general, sativa strains tend to be heavier on the THC. If you don't want to get "high" in the traditional sense, look instead for strains with very low THC and high CBD percentages (see the chart on page 14).

CBD (cannabidiol) is the primary non-psychoactive compound in the cannabis plant that is responsible for a vast array of therapeutic effects, and which has been proved to help alleviate a multitude of ailments without the "high." The beauty of CBD is that it is well tolerated and safe even at high doses. CBD is commonly referred to as the "medicine" in the cannabis plant, and scientists and researchers have been successfully showing that CBD oil shrinks tumors, quells seizures, eases chronic pain, and treats the symptoms of many ailments, including fibromyalgia, PMS, joint and muscle pain, and spasms. Scientists from Israel have even proved that CBD also helps heal and strengthen broken bones. In general, indica strains tend to have higher percentages of CBD.

Each cannabis strain has a different ratio of cannabinoids that provides different effects, which is why the experience differs from one strain to another. It's important to note that the chemical profile of many sativa strains is THC dominant, while the chemical profile of many indica strains is more balanced and has a higher percentage of CBD. That being said, most indica strains are still very low in CBD. For medicinal purposes, it's imperative to use specific strains that are known to be high in CBD. Charlotte's Web, ACDC, Sour Tsunami, Harlequin, and Harle-Tsu are some of the highest-CBD strains (and happen to be sativa or sativa-dominant hybrids). The best medicinal cannabis strains combine both THC and CBD along with terpenes and flavonoids (more on these elements below) to provide whole plant therapeutics, or what is known as the "entourage effect." The entourage effect is the cumulative result of the interaction of all the cannabinoid compounds.

The THC:CBD ratio and purported entourage effect are the two most important things to look for when you are medicating with cannabis. Your dispensary should be able to tell you the THC:CBD ratio of each strain, and a knowledgeable "bud tender" or a search of leafly.com can provide you with an overview of each strain's known effects. For medicinal cooking and baking, it is ideal to use strains that have high levels of CBD. While most strains currently have very low levels of CBD, this is changing rapidly, as more and more patients turn to medical marijuana and seek high-CBD strains. Most dispensaries now carry at least one or two CBD-rich strains. For recreational users, the CBD:THC ratio is not that important. What is important is finding a strain that has a reputation for imparting your desired psychoactive outcome. Do you want to feel happy, euphoric, giddy, and uplifted? Then you want a strain like Sour Diesel, Jack Herer, or any strain whose name ends with the word *Haze* (*Haze* is used to refer to sativa-dominant strains). If you prefer more of a relaxed body high, you'll want a strain like Blue Dream, Girl Scout Cookies, or any strain whose name ends with the word *Kush*.

Other Elements

There are a few other important elements and compounds to consider when it comes to understanding cannabis plants. Trichomes are the beautiful crystal-like resin glands you see on your flower or "bud." Trichomes are hydrophobic and cannot be washed off the plant–and that's lucky for us, because this is where the cannabis plant stores all of its THC and CBD. Terpenes and flavonoids are responsible for variations in the plant's smell and flavor profile, and they also have certain medicinal properties of their own. Along with THC and CBD, terpenes and flavonoids contribute to the overall effect of a strain. Though they are the lesser-known compounds within cannabis plants, researchers are uncovering the increasingly important role they play alongside the more popular elements of THC and CBD.

Beneficial Effects

Cannabinoids affect the human body by interacting with different receptors and regulatory enzymes within the endocannabinoid system (ECS), a complex signaling network that has widespread effects within the body. The following chart (page 10) provides an introduction to some of the main cannabis compounds and their corresponding effects.

As you can see, CBD provides a vast array of health benefits. Because it is non-psychoactive and can be given in large doses with few to no side effects, it has been used effectively as an anti-psychotic. CBD has consistently demonstrated neuroprotective effects and seems to have strong anti-cancer potential. Recent research points to the powerful impact of CBD on cancer cells, whereby it arrests cell division, migration, metastasis, and invasiveness. Some scientists are hopeful CBD could relegate chemotherapy and radiation to second and third options for cancer patients. After years of restrictions on cannabis research in the United States, researchers feel this is just the beginning in terms of unlocking the medicinal benefits of CBDs.

Side Effects

Regardless of your edible goals, make sure you research the strains of cannabis you're planning to cook with and understand their purported entourage effect before you buy them. A reputable cannabis health center with educated bud tenders can give you this information, but leafly.com is a great resource for those who don't have access to proper centers. The more you know, the better your experience and intended outcome will be.

In addition, when consuming any drug or herbal remedy, you should be educated and aware of all potential side effects–and cannabis is no different.

BENEFICIAL EFFECTS

△9−THC	Reduces vomiting and nausea
	Stimulates appetite
	Relieves pain
	Suppresses muscle spasms
△9−THCA	Aids sleep
	Inhibits cancer cell growth
	Suppresses muscle spasms
△8−THC	Relieves pain
THCV	Reduces convulsions and seizures
	Promotes bone growth
CBD	Acts as an antibacterial
	Balances function in the immune system
	Inhibits cancer cell growth
	Provides neuroprotection
	Promotes bone growth
	Reduces seizures and convulsions
	Reduces blood sugar levels
	Reduces inflammation
	Reduces risk of artery blockage
	Reduces small intestine contractions
	Reduces vomiting and nausea
	Relieves pain
	Relieves anxiety
	Slows bacterial growth
	Suppresses muscle spasms
	Tranquilizes
	Treats psoriasis
	Decreases vascular pressure

CBDA	Reduces inflammation
	Inhibits cancer cell growth
CBG	Aids sleep
	Inhibits cancer cell growth
	Promotes bone growth
	Slows bacterial growth
CBGA	Reduces inflammation
	Relieves pain
	Slows bacterial growth
CBC	Inhibits cancer cell growth
	Promotes bone growth
	Reduces inflammation
	Relieves pain

*Source: *https://patients4medicalmarijuana.wordpress.com/2013/04/26/cbd-unprecedented-healing-power/*.

According to MedlinePlus, the National Institutes of Health's website produced by the National Library of Medicine, "Marijuana intoxication rarely needs medical advice or treatment. Occasionally, serious symptoms occur. These symptoms are rare and usually associated with other drugs or compounds mixed in with marijuana."

Fortunately, no one has ever died from cannabis intoxication, as cannabis is not "toxic" to the human body. Still, side effects related to cannabis consumption can include dry mouth, short-term memory issues, disorientation, red eyes, fatigue, slower reaction times, reduced motor coordination, sensory distortion, high blood pressure, headaches, increased heart rate, paranoia, and anxiety.

Cannabis is a medicine and should be treated the same way you would treat any other medicine. This is why it is important for you to understand what you are cooking and/or baking with and to dose your edibles properly to ensure that you and those you cook for have an enjoyable experience . . . especially after the fact. Guests may love your food, but if they have too much cannabis, it will come back to haunt them (and you!) several hours later. It is also important that your guests do not smoke marijuana before or during your meal. It's difficult to track the amount of cannabis you've consumed if you're smoking on top of eating edibles—and too much cannabis can lead to undesirable and unpleasant side effects such as anxiety, paranoia, insomnia, and an unwelcome weed hangover the next day.

If that should happen, though, have no fear. Try popping an ibuprofen or two, which helps with the unpleasant side effects of cannabis. A study in the journal *Cell* showed that ibuprofen can help get rid of the THC high while still maintaining the health benefits. Scientists found that when they blocked an enzyme called COX-2 (which ibuprofen does), the high disappeared (along with the neurological side effects), while the treatment benefits of THC remained.

POPULAR STRAINS
& EFFECTS

FOR THOSE WHO are dedicated to cooking and baking with high-CBD strains, the following chart lists the most popular high-CBD strains and their CBD and THC percentage ranges. Since the potency of each "grow" depends on the conditions and methods used for growing, the CBD and THC profile will vary with each batch. Check with your dispensary to get the actual percentages of CBD and THC in your flower.

STRAIN	SPECIES	CBD%	THC%	CBD:THC	USED FOR
Cannatonic	Hybrid	0–23.4%	0–14%	1:1	Helps alleviate pain, inflammation, muscle spasms, stress, depression
Harlequin	Sativa-dominant hybrid	8–16%	4–7%	5:2	Helps alleviate pain, inflammation, fibromyalgia,* PMS,* anxiety, stress, depression; to counteract paranoia
Charlotte's Web	Sativa	20%	0–0.5%	20:<1	Helps alleviate seizures, pain, stress, depression, headaches
Sour Tsunami	Sativa-dominant hybrid	0–11%	0–10%	1:1	Helps alleviate pain, inflammation, muscle spasms, fatigue, stress
Harle-Tsu	Sativa-dominant hybrid	0–6.4%	0–9.5%	2:1	Helps alleviate pain, inflammation, fibromyalgia, ADHD, anxiety, depression

Sources: *leafly.com, verdabase.com. *Although this is not specifically listed on leafly, I have found through personal experience with patients that these conditions are helped by this strain.*

CANNATONIC

HARLEQUIN

If you prefer to cook or bake with high-THC strains, you can find many of the following popular strains at most dispensaries.

STRAIN	SPECIES	THC%	PURPORTED EFFECTS	USED FOR
Blue Dream	Sativa-dominant hybrid	17–24%	Happy, relaxed, euphoric, uplifted, creative	Helps alleviate stress, depression, pain, insomnia, headaches
OG Kush	Sativa	9–25%	Happy, uplifted, euphoric, energetic, creative	Helps alleviate stress, depression, pain, fatigue, loss of appetite
Sour Diesel	Indica-dominant hybrid	19–26%	Relaxed, happy, euphoric, uplifted, hungry	Helps alleviate migraines, ADD/ADHD, stress, depression, pain, insomnia
Jack Herrer	Sativa	18–23%	Happy, euphoric, uplifted, energetic, creative	Helps alleviate stress, depression, pain, fatigue, loss of appetite
Girl Scout Cookies	Indica-dominant hybrid	17–28%	Happy, relaxed, euphoric, uplifted, creative	Helps alleviate stress, depression, pain, loss of appetite, insomnia

THE ART OF COOKING WITH CANNABIS

COOKING WITH CANNABIS *is both an art and a science.*
The art is in cooking and baking food so that it tastes and looks great.
The science is in choosing the right strain of cannabis to achieve your
desired results and then dosing your edibles properly. Bring them both
together, and you've got yourself a successful edible experience.

There is a lot of important information about both the art and the
science of cooking with cannabis in the following pages, and I promise
to keep things fun as I break it all down for you.

The Basics

KNOW YOUR PERCENTAGES

When you are cooking and baking with cannabis, it is critically important to know the percentage of THC and CBD in the flower (or bud) you are using to infuse your butters and oils. If you shop at a reputable dispensary or health center, it will be able to give you this information. Thus, it's fairly easy to get this information in locales such as Northern California, Colorado, Oregon, and Washington State, where dispensaries and health centers are required to disclose this information— but outside of these locations, it's a gamble. Another reason to shop at reputable dispensaries and health centers is to ensure that you get what you pay for. The best dispensaries are steadfast when it comes to quality and strain integrity, as they stake their reputations on it. If shopping at a good dispensary is not an option where you live, look up the strain you are interested in on leafly.com or allbud.com and use the "mean" of the strain's potency range to estimate the percentage of THC and CBD in your herb. For a list of recommended reputable dispensaries, you can visit my website, jeffthe420chef.com.

ACTIVATION AND INFUSION

As it turns out, neither THC nor CBD is active in raw cannabis. THC comes from tetrahydrocannabinolic acid (THCA) and CBD comes from cannabidiolic acid (CBDA). These two acids are the precursors to THC and CBD, found in raw, live cannabis, but neither has any active properties on its own. Both THC and CBD need to be "activated" through a process called "decarbing" (decarboxylation) before their effects can be felt. Essentially, decarbing means removing the acid, or the "A" molecule, from the THC and CBD, which happens by releasing a carbon atom from a carbon chain. This can be done only through heat and time. When you smoke cannabis, you decarb the bud via heat before it goes into your lungs. But in order to cook with cannabis, you need to "activate" the THC and CBD by decarbing your bud before you can infuse it into your food.

THC and CBD, along with the other natural compounds (cannabinoids) in raw cannabis, are *hydrophobic*, meaning they cannot be infused into water. They are fat-soluble, however, which means that they can be infused into ingredients containing high levels of fat, such as butter and oil. In the coming pages, I will show you (1) how to decarb your cannabis to activate the THC and CBD, and (2) how to infuse those compounds into butters and oils. I recommend using healthy fats and oils (such as grass-fed butter, coconut oil, and olive oil) for the best results.

DELIVERY METHOD AND "KICK-IN" TIME

THC and CBD need to be digested and metabolized before you can experience their effects. And it's important to keep in mind that everybody metabolizes edible cannabis differently. But since it takes less time to digest a liquid than a solid, the THC and/or CBD in a salad dressing will hit you much faster than that in a dense edible like a brownie. When cannabis is actually *baked* into an item, that item must first be digested before the THC and/or CBD can be metabolized. So as a general rule of thumb, "kick-in" time is determined primarily by how the cannabis is introduced into the body.

SETUP IS KEY

The French culinary term *mise en place* means "everything in its place," and the idea is crucial to creating great-tasting, precisely dosed edibles and meals with very little stress. *Mise en place*, which is all about staging and having everything ready at your fingertips, is the foundation of every successful chef and restaurant. Make sure that you have all your ingredients, utensils, and appliances set up, prepped, measured, organized, and ready to go before you start cooking or baking. And there is a bonus that comes with this preparation: once you have mastered *mise en place* in the kitchen, it somehow permeates everything else you do. As it becomes habit, life becomes simpler, more organized, and less chaotic overall.

COOKING TIMES AND TEMPS

Since the compounds in cannabis can be easily vaporized or destroyed, it's important to be aware of the temperature you use when cooking edibles, and the amount of time for which you cook things. Although THC begins to evaporate at 355°F and CBD at 392°F, I have found that the optimal temperature for cooking and baking with cannabis is 340°F for recipes requiring 1 hour or less. For recipes that require over 1 hour of cooking or baking time, 325°F is optimal.

MEASUREMENTS FOR MEALS

To give a general idea of the THC potency of each dish, all of the recipes show the approximate milligrams of THC per serving. These calculations are based on popular cannabis strains of 10%, 15%, and 20% THC, and are included to provide ballpark estimates only. Please note that these numbers will differ based on the strain you use and that strain's specific percentage of THC, so you will have to calculate your own milligrams per serving using the formula on page 28 (or you can use the THC/CBD calculator on my website, jeffthe420chef.com).

To reiterate, it's important to pay close attention to how much THC you put in your recipe. While you can't have too much CBD, you *can* have too much THC. The negative psychoactive effects of too much THC (amplified anxiety, mood changes, paranoia, and morning nausea and grogginess) will lead to a very unpleasant experience for everyone. For 420 *meals*, you must cut the amount of canna-butter or canna-oil in each recipe (see Controlling Potency below) to ensure that your meal is properly dosed.

CONTROLLING POTENCY

When it comes to enjoying a full 420 meal and/or more than one mouthwatering edible, I have found that "low dosing" THC is the secret. Low dosing means that you use less THC-infused butter or oil for each recipe, which allows you to enjoy safely more of the great-tasting food that you make.

You accomplish low dosing by cutting the potency of the butter or oil in your recipe. To control the potency of your edibles, you will first need to know the percentage of THC and CBD in your starting canna-butter or canna-oil. From there, you can calculate how much *non-infused* butter or oil you need to mix in to achieve your desired potency per serving. I've included a chart in the coming pages to help with these calculations.

Colorado's Marijuana Enforcement Division has set the standard dose of edible cannabis at 10 milligrams of THC. There is no set standard for CBD. For most people, 10 milligrams of THC will feel like enjoying two glasses of wine or two beers. I typically start my dinner parties at around 5 milligrams of THC per person and take them up to a total of 10 to 15 by dessert, but it all depends on the guests' individual tolerance levels. My general policy is that I won't take anyone past 20 milligrams of THC. It's good practice to check in regularly with your guests to ensure that they are having an enjoyable experience and to modify what you serve each guest, if necessary.

TASTE

It took me almost two years to perfect my light-tasting canna-butter and canna-oil recipes. The following four steps are my secret to neutralizing much of the cannabis taste so that you can create great-tasting edibles. (Please note that this process will be described again in greater detail in the opening recipes for canna-butter and canna-oil.)

1. Soak, Blanch, and Rinse. The first secret to creating "light-tasting" canna-butter and canna-oils is to grind your herb coarsely, soak it for 24 to 48 hours in distilled water (the longer the soak, the cleaner the herb), and then blanch it. Blanching is a cooking process that involves placing fruits, vegetables, and herbs in boiling water for a short period of time and then quickly halting the cooking process by submerging the item in ice water to shock it back or refresh it. Chefs do this to cook partially or soften fruits and vegetables, but a longer blanch will also help remove strong tastes from foods like garlic and onion. Since THC, CBD, and many other cannabinoids are hydrophobic, meaning they won't dissolve in water, I realized that this was a great way to remove some of the taste of cannabis while also deep cleaning the bud.

To blanch your herb, simply place it in boiling water for 5 minutes to get rid of any remaining impurities, and then immediately place it in a bowl of ice water for a minute to stop the cooking process. Blanching removes much of the non-chemical compounds (chlorophyll, pistils, pesticides, and microbiological contaminants like mold and bacteria) that contribute to the taste that is present in most cannabis-infused edibles. To ensure your herb is as clean as possible, you'll want to rinse the blanched herb with distilled water before you decarb and dry it as well.

2. Decarb and Dry. Decarbing and drying your herb overnight is the next essential step in removing a lot of the taste. Wet or damp cannabis, even after soaking and blanching, will still impart the flavors stuck in the moisture. As I mentioned earlier, the THC and CBD need to be "activated" through a process called decarbing before their effects can be felt. To decarb your cannabis after blanching and drying, place it in the oven at 300°F for 20 minutes. *Note:* You will lose up to 30% to 50% of your cannabis weight through this process, depending on how fresh your cannabis is to start.

3. Simmer and Steep. A French coffee press is the perfect infusion container for this next stage in the process. Just add your butter or oil to the French press along with your blanched, dried, and decarbed cannabis. Cover the French press, push the plunger till it meets the top of your butter or oil, and place it in a pot of boiling water for 3 to 4 hours. The pot should be filled with enough water to hit just above the butter or oil line in the French press. The French press method keeps the infusion environment pure and the temperature constant. And since the French press has a built-in strainer, you don't need to use cheesecloth to strain everything at the end. The French press also does a wonderful job of separating the milk solids, which basically creates canna-ghee or cannabis-infused clarified butter. After the steep, just push the plunger in the French press all the way down and pour your butter or oil into a dish or container for storage and use. *Note:* You will lose up to 25% of your butter or oil volume through this process.

4. Cut. You can cut the taste and lower the dosage of your resulting canna-butter and canna-oil simply by combining it with non-infused butter or oil. Start by determining the amount of cannabis you want in your recipe, and use the appropriate amount of canna-butter or canna-oil to achieve that amount. Then add non-infused butter or oil to make up the difference. See the chart on page 27 for a general idea as to how many milligrams of THC or CBD are in various strengths and quantities of canna-butter and canna-oil.

The Rules of Hosting 420 Meals

Here are a few things to be aware of and to plan for as the host or chef of cannabis-infused meals:

1. **Ask your guests not to smoke cannabis before or during your meal.** Let the experience be all about your edibles. If your guests smoke before or during your meal, you will be layering additional THC on top of what they have already consumed, which can lead to anxiety, paranoia, and an uncomfortable period for them—and for you.

2. **A little wine is okay . . . at the beginning.** One or two glasses of wine with a meal is fine, but anything beyond that can be problematic—as can other alcoholic beverages. Wine is okay because of its relatively low alcohol content. There are two reasons to limit your alcoholic consumption so strictly while consuming edibles. First, you want your guests to experience the effects of the cannabis in your edibles and not to confuse what they feel from the alcohol with what they feel from the cannabis. The other reason is more scientific. Research studies have shown that consuming alcohol with cannabis almost doubles the THC levels in the blood, which increases the "high" and makes the psychoactive effects more pronounced. Cooking or baking with cannabis is a science as much as a culinary art, and if you drink or allow your guests to drink more than a glass or two of wine, you run the risk of the negative side effects from overmedicating.

3. **Make sure your guests have some *non-infused* food in their stomachs before you begin.** Consuming cannabis-infused edibles on an empty stomach can magnify the effects of the THC and lead to undesirable side effects such as nausea, anxiety, and paranoia. An easy way to prevent that is by consuming a non-infused snack before eating edibles.

4. **Provide non-infused food for balance.** It's a good idea to have non-infused fare—be it offering menu items prepared both with and without cannabis or providing other selections entirely—at your meals. This helps your guests choose just how much cannabis they want to ingest at your meal, without leaving them hungry.

5. **Start early.** Keep in mind that everyone metabolizes cannabis-infused edibles differently, and that it can take anywhere from 30 minutes to 3 hours to feel the effects. It's best to keep your schedule open a few hours after a 420 meal to provide ample time to appreciate the benefits.

To expand on this last point, it will often take more time than you've expected or planned for the effects of edibles to be felt. About a year ago, I cooked for a group of executives in Colorado who decided that a 420 dinner would be a great way to bond with their new CEO, a large, gruff man. For the first few hours, everyone except the CEO was having a great time, while he remained straight-faced and quiet. It wasn't until 3 hours later that someone said something that triggered a huge guffaw from the CEO. Soon, he was laughing so hard that he fell off his chair. So don't sweat it if things are not happening as fast as you hoped. You should also be aware that a small number of people lack the enzyme responsible for metabolizing the compounds found in cannabis (and therefore are immune to the benefits).

HOW TO USE
THIS COOKBOOK

IN THIS SECTION, you will find two important calculators to use when cooking and baking with cannabis. The first calculator will help you figure out the potency of your canna-butters or canna-oils after you infuse them (i.e., it will tell you how many milligrams of THC or CBD are in your canna-butter or canna-oil). The second calculator will help you figure out the potency of each recipe and serving based on the canna-butter or canna-oil used (i.e., it will tell you how many milligrams of THC or CBD are in each recipe and serving).

Due to volume lost during the infusion process, you won't end up with the same amount of butter or oil as you started with. Here's a handy chart showing the conversion of various measurements of butter and oil, from starting quantities to post-infusion quantities. For example, if you want to end up with 1 stick of canna-butter, you need to start with 1⅓ sticks of butter to account for what's lost during infusion.

BUTTER CONVERSION CHART

	INFUSE
For 1 stick of canna-butter	1⅓ sticks of butter
For 1 lb. canna-butter (4 sticks)	5⅓ sticks of butter
For 4 oz. canna-oil	5 oz. oil
For 8 oz. canna-oil	10 oz. oil
For 16 oz. canna-oil	20 oz. oil

THE CALCULATORS TAKE INTO ACCOUNT THE FOLLOWING:

1. You will lose approximately 20% of your oil volume and 25% of your butter volume in the infusion process. You lose more butter because the water and milk solids in the butter will be lost, along with whatever still sticks to the plant material.

2. When you use my method, your cured and decarbed cannabis will weigh +/−20% to +/−50% *less* than your starting weight, depending on how moist or dry your starting product was. If your product was very dry, you may lose only 20% (+/−).

How to Calculate THC/CBD in Canna-Butter and Canna-Oil

Estimating the amount of THC and/or CBD in your canna-butter and canna-oil is critical when it comes to cooking and baking with cannabis. The formula below, developed with CW Analytical (cwanalytical.com), will help you calculate approximately how many milligrams of THC and CBD your infused butter or oil will contain. When making butters and oils, please refer to this formula to get an accurate calculation—or you can use the simple THC/CBD calculator on my website (jeffthe420chef.com).

CALCULATOR FOR INFUSION OF CANNA-BUTTER & CANNA-OIL

STEP 1: Enter the starting THC percentage or CBD percentage from the strain you're using (you'll need to calculate both separately if you want to measure both). As a reminder, you can't have too much CBD, but you *can* have too much THC:

_____ %

STEP 2: Weigh your *final* decarbed and dried cannabis (this will likely be considerably less than your starting weight):

_____ grams

STEP 3: Convert the amount of butter or oil you started with into grams (see gram conversion chart on page 29):

_____ grams

STEP 4: Multiply your starting THC % or CBD % (from Step 1) by 0.5 to account for loss due to the decarbing and drying process:

_____ final %

STEP 5A: BUTTER: Multiply the grams of your starting amount of butter (from Step 3) by 0.75 to account for a 25% volume loss of butter during infusion:

_____ grams

STEP 5B: OIL: Multiply the grams of your starting amount of oil (from Step 3) by 0.8 to account for a 20% volume loss of oil during infusion:

_____ grams

How to Calculate THC/CBD per Recipe and per Serving

Estimating the amount of THC and/or CBD per serving of food is critical when it comes to cooking and baking with cannabis. The formula below will tell you approximately how many milligrams of THC and CBD you'll be serving and/or consuming with each edible. When making edibles, please refer to this formula to get an accurate calculation—or you can use the simple THC/CBD calculator on my website (jeffthe420chef.com).

CALCULATOR FOR COOKING & BAKING WITH CANNABIS

STEP 1: Enter amount of canna-butter or canna-oil called for in your recipe in grams (see gram conversion chart on page 29): _____ **grams**

STEP 2: To convert grams to milligrams, multiply your final THC % or CBD % (from Step 4 of canna-butter/canna-oil calculator) by 10 to determine the number of milligrams per gram of THC or CBD. (For example, a strain of 20% THC means the cannabis is 20% THC per gram. In order to transfer that into milligrams, you multiply by 10 and get 200mg/g of THC.): _____ **THC or CBD mg/g**

STEP 3: Multiply THC or CBD mg/g (from Step 2 above) by your final cannabis weight after decarbing and drying (from Step 2 of canna-butter/canna-oil calculator): _____ **Total mg of THC or CBD**

STEP 4: Divide total mg of THC or CBD (from Step 3 above) by grams of butter or oil you are infusing (from Step 3 of canna-butter/canna-oil calculator): _____ **mg/g THC or CBD in butter or oil**

STEP 5: Multiply mg/g of THC or CBD (from Step 4 above) by grams of butter or oil in your recipe (Step 1 above): _____ **mg THC or CBD in recipe**

STEP 6: Divide mg THC or CBD in recipe (from Step 5 above) by number of servings called for in the recipe: _____ **mg THC or CBD/serving**

STEP 7 **FOR OIL ONLY:** Multiply total number of mg THC or CBC/serving (from Step 6 above) by 1.2 to account for 20% increased potency in oil: _____ **mg THC or CBD/serving for oil**

GRAM CONVERSIONS—MEASUREMENT CHART

BUTTER

Quantity	Tablespoons	Grams
1 ⅓ sticks	10.6	151
1 stick	8	113.4
1 cup	16	226.8
¾ cup	12	170.1
½ cup	8	113.4
¼ cup	4	56.7
1 tablespoon	1	14.18

OIL

Quantity	Tablespoons	Grams
5 fluid ounces	10	137
1 cup	16	219.55
¾ cup	12	164.67
½ cup	8	109.78
¼ cup	4	54.89
1 fluid ounce	2	27.44
1 tablespoon	1	13.72

To make it easy for you, I've prepared the following charts to help you figure out, at a glance, approximately how many milligrams of THC or CBD are in your recipe, based on the amount of canna-butter or canna-oil you use in your recipe and the percentage of THC and/or CBD in your starting bud (before curing and processing). I've calculated the average loss factor at 30%.

APPROXIMATE MILLIGRAMS OF THC OR CBD PER SERVING
(some numbers have been rounded)

Canna-butter called for in recipe	2 servings THC or CBD %: mg	4 servings THC or CBD %: mg	6 servings THC or CBD %: mg	8 servings THC or CBD %: mg	12 servings THC or CBD %: mg
1 teaspoon	10%: 3.8 15%: 5.9 20%: 7.5	10%: 1.9 15%: 3.2 20%: 3.8	10%: 1.3 15%: 1.9 20%: 2.6	—	—
1 tablespoon	10%: 11.5 15%: 17.0 20%: 23.0	10%: 5.7 15%: 8.5 20%: 11.5	10%: 3.8 15%: 5.7 20%: 7.6	10%: 2.8 15%: 4.3 20%: 5.6	10%: 1.9 15%: 2.8 20%: 3.8
¼ cup or ½ stick	10%: 46.0 15%: 69.3 20%: 92.0	10%: 23.0 15%: 34.6 20%: 46.2	10%: 15.4 15%: 23.0 20%: 30.8	10%: 11.5 15%: 17.3 20%: 23.0	10%: 7.7 15%: 11.5 20%: 15.4
½ cup or 1 stick	10%: 92.5 15%: 138.0 20%: 185.0	10%: 46.2 15%: 69.3 20%: 92.4	10%: 30.8 15%: 46.2 20%: 61.6	10%: 23.0 15%: 34.6 20%: 46.0	10%: 15.4 15%: 23.0 20%: 31.8
1 cup or 2 sticks	10%: 185.0 15%: 277.3 20%: 370.0	10%: 92.5 15%: 138.6 20%: 185.0	10%: 61.6 15%: 92.4 20%: 123.2	10%: 46.2 15%: 69.3 20%: 92.4	10%: 30.8 15%: 46.2 20%: 61.6
Creamy Canna-Butter (page 44)	Divide mg above by 2	Divide mg above by 2	Divide mg above by 2	Divide mg above by 2	Divide mg above by 2

Canna-oil called for in recipe	2 servings THC or CBD %: mg	4 servings THC or CBD %: mg	6 servings THC or CBD %: mg	8 servings THC or CBD %: mg	12 servings THC or CBD %: mg
1 teaspoon	10%: 5.0 15%: 7.6 20%: 10.0	10%: 2.5 15%: 3.8 20%: 5.0	10%: 1.6 15%: 2.5 20%: 3.2	—	—
1 tablespoon	10%: 15.2 15%: 22.8 20%: 30.4	10%: 7.6 15%: 11.4 20%: 16.2	10%: 5.0 15%: 7.6 20%: 10.0	10%: 3.8 15%: 5.7 20%: 7.6	10%: 2.5 15%: 3.8 20%: 5.0
¼ cup	10%: 60.9 15%: 91.4 20%: 121.8	10%: 30.4 15%: 45.7 20%: 60.8	10%: 20.3 15%: 30.4 20%: 40.6	10%: 15.2 15%: 22.8 20%: 30.4	10%: 10.1 15%: 15.2 20%: 20.2
½ cup	10%: 121.9 15%: 182.8 20%: 243.8	10%: 60.9 15%: 91.4 20%: 121.8	10%: 40.6 15%: 60.9 20%: 81.2	10% 30.4 15%: 45.7 20%: 60.8	10%: 20.3 15%: 30.4 20%: 40.6
1 cup	10%: 243.8 15%: 365.7 20%: 487.6	10%: 121.8 15%: 182.8 20%: 243.6	10%: 81.2 15%: 121.9 20%: 162.4	10%: 60.8 15%: 91.4 20%: 121.6	10%: 40.6 15%: 60.9 20%: 81.2

· PART ·

2

Recipes

Butters & Oils

Infusing Butters and Oils

BUTTER

I highly recommend using grass-fed butter for all of your cooking needs (my favorite brand is Kerrygold). The difference between grass-fed butter and regular butter comes through in the quality of the butter and how good it is for you. Grass-fed butter contains vitamins A, E, and K_2. Vitamin K is important for heart health, and K_2 is what keeps calcium out of your arteries and in your bones. Grass-fed butter is also rich in conjugated linoleic acid (CLA), a fatty acid that has powerful health benefits. Although the jury is still out, numerous studies have shown that CLA may actually lower body fat percentages. In addition, grass-fed butter contains butyrate, a short-chain fatty acid that has been proved to fight inflammation and improve stomach health.

OILS

The following oils are the best (and healthiest) to use for THC/CBD infusion:

Coconut oil	Avocado oil	Sesame oil	Almond oil
Olive oil	Peanut oil	Walnut oil	

Always aim to use tested cannabis when making your own butters and oils. Ask the dispensary or cultivator from whom you are procuring your cannabis for test results—for potency, and also for pesticides and microbiological contaminants like mold and bacteria. Or you can test your cannabis flower in the comfort of your home with MyDX, a portable chemical analyzer that identifies the composition of your cannabis. If you don't have access to a testing lab or to cannabis that has been tested, you can roughly determine the potency of your butter or oil by visiting leafly.com or allbud.com to estimate the starting potency of your cannabis strain. Most strains can be estimated as having anywhere from 10% to 20% THC, depending on factors like exposure to the sun, exposure to the elements, and strain genetics. If you're not sure of the amount of THC in your strain, a good rule of thumb is to estimate it at 15–18%.

If possible, you should test your butter or oil after making it to ensure that you've processed it correctly and haven't experienced major losses in CBD or THC. This can be done quickly and fairly inexpensively. Reputable labs offer discounted testing to individual patients looking to test their personal-use medicine.*

Information contributed by CW Analytical (cwanalytical.com).

"LIGHT-TASTING" CANNA-BUTTER

My "light-tasting" canna-butter is the basis of many of my guests' favorite dishes. This is more of a bright yellow ghee (clarified butter) with a hint of green, and it's perfect for baking and cooking light and healthy dishes with cannabis. It is also the base ingredient for my "Light-Tasting" Creamy Canna-Butter (page 44). To soften canna-butter, leave at room temperature for 30 minutes.

WHAT YOU'LL NEED

Distilled water

Tea strainer (large)

Medium-/large-sized pot

Bowl filled with ice water

French press coffeemaker

Heat-resistant glass dish or baking tin

Aluminum foil

Plastic butter dish with cover

INGREDIENTS

¼ ounce (7 grams) cannabis flower

1⅓ sticks butter (10½ tablespoons), salted or unsalted (I prefer grass-fed, and my favorite brand is Kerrygold)

recipe continues

SERVINGS

1

stick of canna-butter = 8 (1-tablespoon) servings

PREP TIME

1

hour and 5 minutes

COOK TIME

3

hours

IDLE TIME

24

hours plus overnight

APPROXIMATE THC PER SERVING*

10%: 23 mg

15%: 34 mg

20%: 46 mg

1   Coarsely grind dry herb (also known as flower or bud) and soak in distilled water for 24–48 hours. Change the water twice a day. This cleans out a lot of the impurities that cause bad taste.

2   The next day, place "cleaned" herb in a tea strainer. Bring water to a boil in a pot. Place tea strainer in boiling water for 5 minutes.

3   Remove tea strainer after 5 minutes, then place in bowl of ice water for 1 minute. Remove from ice water and pour distilled water over the tea strainer to rinse out any residual impurities. Remove herb from strainer and wring out excess water.

4   Spread blanched and squeezed cannabis evenly in a large baking pan and lay a large piece of aluminum foil loosely on top of it (i.e., don't crimp it down tightly around the edges). Let it sit overnight. Your cannabis should be dry by the next morning. You can skip this step if you use a dehydrator.

5   When dry, preheat oven to 300°F.

6   Now, crimp down the foil and "bake" for 20 minutes. (This is how you decarb your cannabis.)

7   Remove from oven. Let sit for 5 minutes so THC and CBD vapors can settle back onto the herb. Remove foil and loosely cover with a couple of paper towels. This creates a dark environment with airflow.

8   Let pan sit, covered with paper towels, on the counter for 2-4 hours to dry out any residual moisture.

NOTE

Your final yield will weigh +/−20% to +/−50% *less* than your starting weight, depending on how moist or dry your cannabis was when you started the process.

STEP 3—INFUSE BUTTER

1   Melt butter in a French press placed standing up in pot of simmering water.

2   Mix decarbed cannabis into melted butter and cover the French press. Press plunger to just above the butter. This will be your water line.

3   Gently simmer for 3 hours. Check the water level every 20 minutes to ensure it is even with or slightly higher than the water line.

4   After 3 hours, remove the French press from the pot, push the plunger all the way down, and strain the butter into a butter container. Refrigerate to resolidify.

5   Remove solidified butter from refrigerator and separate from butter dish onto a paper towel. This will remove any residual water that accumulated from the process. Dry carefully by blotting your butter with a paper towel to remove as much moisture as possible.

6   Place back in butter dish and use within 1 month.

Approximate dose per serving is based on infusing 5 grams of cured/dried/decarbed cannabis into 1⅓ sticks of butter.

"LIGHT-TASTING" CREAMY CANNA-BUTTER

For creamy canna-butter, you have to reintroduce the milk solids. This is an easy process—just whisk together equal parts softened "light-tasting" canna-butter and grass-fed butter.

1 stick "light-tasting" canna-butter, softened

1 stick grass-fed butter, softened

1   In a large bowl, whisk the "light-tasting" canna-butter and butter together until creamy and smooth. Refrigerate to resolidify or use as is.

2   Use within 2 weeks.

Approximate dose per serving is based on infusing 5 grams of cured/dried/decarbed cannabis into 1⅓ sticks of butter.

NOTE
With this recipe, your creamy canna-butter will be *half as potent* as your starting "light-tasting" canna-butter. This is a great option if you want to make delicious, low-dose baked goods (because let's face it, who wants to eat just one cookie!).

SERVINGS
16
1-tablespoon servings

PREP TIME
35
minutes. 30 minutes to soften butters and 5 minutes to combine.

APPROXIMATE THC PER SERVING*

10%: 11.5 mg

15%: 17 mg

20%: 23 mg

"LIGHT-TASTING" CANNA-OIL

Although there are many oils you can use for infusing cannabis, healthy, high-fat cooking and finishing oils are key to a great-tasting and physically satisfying edible experience. My favorites are coconut, olive, sesame, walnut, and avocado.

WHAT YOU'LL NEED

Distilled water

Tea strainer

Medium/large pot

Bowl filled with ice water

French press coffeemaker

Heat-resistant glass dish or baking tin

Aluminum foil

Glass jar

INGREDIENTS

¼ ounce (7 grams) cannabis

5 ounces oil

STEP 1—SOAK AND BLANCH HERB

1   Coarsely grind dry herb (also known as flower or bud) and soak in distilled water for 24–48 hours. Change the water twice a day. This cleans out a lot of the impurities that cause bad taste.

2   The next day, place "cleaned" herb in a tea strainer. Bring water to a boil in pot. Place tea strainer in boiling water for 5 minutes.

3   Remove tea strainer after 5 minutes, then place in bowl of ice water for 1 minute. Remove from ice water and pour distilled water over the tea strainer to rinse out any residual impurities. Remove herb from strainer and wring out excess water.

SERVINGS

8

1-tablespoon servings

PREP TIME

10

minutes

COOK TIME

4

hours

IDLE TIME

24

hours plus overnight

APPROXIMATE THC PER SERVING*

10%:	30.4 mg
15%:	45.7 mg
20%:	60.8 mg

recipe continues

1   Spread cannabis evenly in a large baking pan and lay a large piece of aluminum foil loosely on top of it (i.e., don't crimp it down tightly around the edges). Let it sit overnight. Your cannabis should be dry by the next morning. You can skip this step if you use a dehydrator.

2   When cannabis is dry, preheat oven to 300°F.

3   Now, crimp down the foil and "bake" for 20 minutes. (This is how you decarb your cannabis.)

4   Remove from oven. Let sit for 5 minutes so THC or CBD vapors can settle back onto the herb. Remove foil and loosely cover with a couple of paper towels. This creates a dark environment with airflow.

5   Let pan sit, covered with paper towels, on the counter for 2–4 hours to dry out any residual moisture.

STEP 3—INFUSE OIL

1   Pour oil into a French press placed standing up in pot of simmering water.

2   Mix decarbed cannabis into oil and cover the French press. Press plunger to just above the oil. This will be your water line.

3   Gently simmer for 4 hours. Check the water level every 20 minutes to ensure it is even with or slightly higher than the water line.

4   After 4 hours, remove the French press from the pot, push the plunger all the way down, and strain the oil into a clean jar. Your final yield should be about 4 ounces.

5   Use immediately or refrigerate for up to 2 weeks. To reliquefy oil that has solidified, place oil container in a pot of hot water for 15–20 minutes.

*Approximate dose per serving is based on infusing 5 grams of cured/dried/decarbed cannabis into 5 ounces of oil.

NOTE

Your final yield will weigh +/−20 to +/−50% *less* than your starting weight, depending on how moist or dry your cannabis was when you started the process.

GARLIC & ROSEMARY CANNA-OIL

Get the party started with this simple and tasty cannabis-infused oil. I love to serve it with fresh pita crisps or Parmesan garlic bread. You can refrigerate it for up to 2 weeks, but it's best during the first week. A word of caution: If you're using this as a dipping oil, it kicks in pretty quickly.

5 fresh rosemary sprigs

¼ cup non-infused olive oil

3 or 4 garlic cloves, minced

¼ cup canna-olive oil

1   Wash and dry rosemary.

2   Pour non-infused oil into a saucepan and heat for 2 minutes. Do not boil. Add garlic and simmer for 2 minutes on low heat.

3   Remove from heat and add in canna-olive oil and rosemary. Let it cool to room temperature. Discard garlic and 4 of the rosemary sprigs.

4   Refrigerate oil with 1 rosemary sprig in a clean, dry bottle. Best if used in the first week but will keep for up to 2 weeks.

5   If oil solidifies in refrigerator, place bottle in pot of hot water for 30–45 minutes to reliquefy.

Approximate dose per serving is based on infusing 5 grams of cured/dried/decarbed cannabis into 5 ounces of oil.

SERVINGS
24
1-teaspoon servings

PREP TIME
5
minutes

COOK TIME
4
minutes

APPROXIMATE THC PER SERVING*

10%: 5 mg

15%: 7.6 mg

20%: 10 mg

HONEY-WHIPPED CANNA-BUTTER

This light and creamy whipped canna-butter is a great topping for pancakes and waffles. But you may find yourself spreading it on a host of other foods as well, given its irresistible taste.

2 tablespoons canna-butter, softened at room temperature for 1 hour

⅔ cup grass-fed butter, softened at room temperature for 1 hour

1½ tablespoons raw honey

1   Whisk together the butters and honey until creamy. Continue to whisk and slowly drizzle in honey until incorporated, rich and creamy.

2   Serve immediately.

Approximate dose per serving is based on infusing 5 grams of cured/dried/decarbed cannabis into 1⅓ sticks of butter.

SERVINGS

12

1-tablespoon servings

PREP TIME

1

hour

COOK TIME

5

hours

APPROXIMATE THC PER SERVING*

10%: 4 mg

15%: 6 mg

20%: 8 mg

Garlic-Dill Canna-
Aioli, page 52

Canna-Cowboy Salsa,
page 64

CHAPTER NO. 2

Sauces & Dips

GARLIC-DILL CANNA-AIOLI

Try this medicated twist on the traditional garlic aioli. Great with burgers or any dish you'd complement with mayonnaise. Serve as a garnish or spread.

2 tablespoons light canna–olive oil

⅔ cup olive oil

3 garlic cloves

2 sprigs dill, finely chopped

2 large egg yolks

4 teaspoons fresh lemon juice

1 teaspoon Dijon mustard

Sea salt

1   Make sure all ingredients and utensils are at room temperature.

2   Combine canna–olive oil with olive oil and mix well.

3   Press garlic and mix with dill.

4   In separate bowl, whisk egg yolks, lemon juice, and mustard.

5   Slowly drizzle oils into egg mixture and whisk vigorously until all the oil is incorporated and aioli is smooth and creamy. If the oil separates, have no fear. Stop adding oil and keep whisking until it's incorporated, then continue.

6   Whisk in the garlic-dill mixture and a pinch or two of salt, until smooth and creamy.

Approximate dose per serving is based on infusing 5 grams of cured/dried/decarbed cannabis into 5 ounces of oil.

SERVINGS

16

1-tablespoon servings

PREP TIME

20

minutes

APPROXIMATE THC PER SERVING*

10%: 3.8 mg

15%: 5.6 mg

20%: 7.6 mg

MOM'S TIP

If your eggs are cold and you want to bring them to room temperature quickly, I learned this great little tip from my mom. Simply put the cold eggs in a bowl, cover them with lukewarm tap water, and let sit for 5 minutes.

SPICY JALAPEÑO CANNA-AIOLI

If you're looking for an aioli with a bit of kick, this is the recipe for you.

2 tablespoons light canna-olive oil

⅔ cup olive oil

1 garlic clove

½ jalapeño pepper, finely minced

2 large egg yolks

4 teaspoons fresh lemon juice

1 teaspoon Dijon mustard

Sea salt

1   Make sure all ingredients and utensils are at room temperature.

2   Combine canna-olive oil with olive oil and mix well.

3   Press garlic and mix with minced jalapeño.

4   In separate bowl, whisk egg yolks, lemon juice, and mustard.

5   Slowly drizzle oils into egg mixture and whisk vigorously until all the oil is incorporated and aioli is smooth and creamy. If the oil separates, have no fear. Stop adding oil and keep whisking until it's incorporated, then continue.

6   Whisk in the garlic-jalapeño mixture and a pinch or two of salt until smooth and creamy.

Approximate dose per serving is based on infusing 5 grams of cured/dried/decarbed cannabis into 5 ounces of oil.

SERVINGS
16
1-tablespoon servings

PREP TIME
20
minutes

APPROXIMATE THC PER SERVING*

10%: 3.8 mg

15%: 5.6 mg

20%: 7.6 mg

LIME-CHIPOTLE CANNA-AIOLI

SERVINGS

16

1-tablespoon
servings

~~~

PREP TIME

20

minutes

~~~

APPROXIMATE
THC PER
SERVING*

10%: 3.8 mg

15%: 5.6 mg

20%: 7.6 mg

This is a great tasty meze to serve alongside my Freaky Fish Tacos (page 186).

2 tablespoons light canna-olive oil

⅔ cup olive oil

1 garlic clove

½ chipotle pepper, canned in adobo sauce, drained and finely minced

2 large egg yolks

4 teaspoons fresh lime juice

1 teaspoon Dijon mustard

Sea salt

1   Make sure all ingredients and utensils are at room temperature.

2   Combine canna–olive oil with olive oil and mix well.

3   Press garlic and mix with minced chipotle pepper.

4   In separate bowl, whisk the egg yolks, lime juice, and mustard.

5   Slowly drizzle the oils into egg mixture and whisk vigorously until all the oil is incorporated and aioli is smooth and creamy. If the oil separates, have no fear. Stop adding oil and keep whisking until it's incorporated, then continue.

6   Whisk in the garlic-chipotle mixture and a pinch or two of salt until smooth and creamy.

Approximate dose per serving is based on infusing 5 grams of cured/dried/decarbed cannabis into 5 ounces of oil.

CANNA-TAHINI

You can enjoy this Canna-Tahini as a great sauce or dressing on its own (try it on roasted vegetables or mix it into a salad) or as a base ingredient for Canna-Hummus (page 56) and Canna-Ghanoush (page 61). Refrigerate for up to one week.

3 cups raw, hulled sesame seeds (unhulled sesame seeds tend to make tahini bitter and grainy)

¼ cup canna-olive oil

¼ cup olive oil (you may not need to use the entire amount, depending on how thin you want your tahini)

¼ cup parsley, minced

1 Preheat oven to 325°F.

2 Spread the sesame seeds evenly onto a large baking sheet. Roast for 6 minutes, shaking pan every minute or so (trust me, it's worth it!). Remove seeds from the oven and let cool for 10 minutes.

3 Place seeds in a food processor and pulse until they become a paste. Continue pulsing while slowly drizzling in the canna–olive oil. Drizzle in olive oil until you reach your desired consistency. When the mixture is smooth and creamy, transfer it from the food processor to a medium bowl.

4 Mix in the parsley and serve with Homemade Pita (page 220) or Canna-Garlic-Infused Pita Chips (page 220).

Approximate dose per serving is based on infusing 5 grams of cured/dried/decarbed cannabis into 5 ounces of oil.

YIELD
2
cups

SERVINGS
32
1-tablespoon servings

PREP TIME
20
minutes

COOK TIME
6
minutes

APPROXIMATE THC PER SERVING*

10%: 3.8 mg

15%: 5.7 mg

20%: 7.6 mg

CANNA-HUMMUS

SERVINGS
24
1-tablespoon
servings

PREP TIME
20
minutes

APPROXIMATE
THC PER
SERVING* (FOR
SUPER−POTENT
VERSION)
10%: 6.2 mg
15%: 9.5 mg
20%: 12.4 mg

Enjoy Canna-Hummus as you would any other hummus. You can make this either "light" or "medium" or "super-potent." For the light version, substitute extra-virgin olive oil for the canna–olive oil. For the medium version, substitute plain tahini for the Canna-Tahini. And for the super-potent, prepare as per the recipe below without substitutions.

2 cups canned chickpeas (one 15-ounce can)

½ cup Canna-Tahini (page 55)

2 tablespoons canna–olive oil, plus 2 tablespoons light olive oil

2 cloves garlic, peeled

2 teaspoons ground cumin

1 teaspoon sweet paprika

Juice of 1 medium lemon

½ teaspoon lemon zest

Salt and freshly ground black pepper

2 to 3 tablespoons parsley (for garnish)

1   Drain the chickpeas over a measuring cup and reserve the liquid.

2   Place the chickpeas, Canna-Tahini, canna-olive oil mixture, garlic, cumin, paprika, lemon juice, lemon zest, and half of the reserved chickpea liquid into a food processor. Pulse to puree. Slowly add in more chickpea liquid until smooth. Add salt and pepper to taste.

3   Garnish with parsley and sprinkle with more paprika before serving.

Approximate dose per serving is based on infusing 5 grams of cured/dried/decarbed cannabis into 5 ounces of oil.

Canna-Harissa, page 60

CANNA-HARISSA

Harissa has always been one of my favorite mezes. This full-bodied, delicately spiced, roasted tomato and pepper hot sauce is not only a tasty dip but also the key ingredient in many delicious North African dishes such as tajine (see Chickpea & Eggplant Canna-Tajine, page 150). Set the stage for a wonderful meal and serve with freshly baked pita alongside Canna-Ghanoush (page 61) and Canna-Hummus (page 56).

SERVINGS
24

PREP TIME
1
hour

COOK TIME
30–40
minutes

APPROXIMATE
THC PER
SERVING*

10%: 2.4 mg

15%: 3.8 mg

20%: 4.8 mg

*Approximate dose per serving is based on infusing 5 grams of cured/dried/decarbed cannabis into 5 ounces of oil.

4 Roma tomatoes

2 sweet red bell peppers

1 serrano pepper

1 chipotle pepper

2 cherry or pimento peppers

4 garlic cloves (2 unpeeled, 2 peeled)

1 teaspoon ground cumin

½ teaspoon ground coriander seeds

½ teaspoon ground caraway seeds

3 teaspoons lemon juice

1 teaspoon sea salt

2 tablespoons canna–olive oil, plus 2 tablespoons light olive oil

½ teaspoon lemon zest

1   Preheat oven to 400°F.

2   Put the tomatoes, peppers, and 2 unpeeled garlic cloves on a baking sheet and roast for 30 to 40 minutes until the peppers and tomatoes are lightly charred and the skin on the garlic cloves is browned. Remove from oven and let cool for 15 to 20 minutes.

3   Once cooled, peel the tomatoes, peppers, and garlic.

4   Place roasted and peeled tomatoes, peppers, and garlic in food processor with the remaining garlic, cumin, coriander, caraway seeds, lemon juice, and salt.

5   Pulse to puree while slowly drizzling in canna-olive oil mixture. Reserve some oil for the end. Scrape down the sides of the food processor if necessary and continue to puree until smooth.

6   Remove from food processor and mix in the lemon zest.

7   Serve immediately as a dip, or pour into a covered container and refrigerate for up to 1 month.

CANNA-GHANOUSH

Baba ghanoush means "pampered papa" in Arabic, and what better way to pamper your guests at the start of a dinner party? Serve with Canna-Chips (page 67) or Poppin' Pita Chips (page 220), and the bowl will be empty in no time.

1 large eggplant, cut lengthwise into 1-inch-thick slices

Sea salt

¼ cup olive oil

¼ cup Canna-Tahini (page 55), plus more as needed

3 garlic cloves, pressed or minced

¼ cup fresh lemon juice, plus more as needed

1 teaspoon lemon zest

½ teaspoon ground cumin

1 tablespoon chopped fresh flat-leaf parsley

1   Preheat oven to 375°F.

2   Poke holes in the eggplant slices. Brush both sides with olive oil and sprinkle each side with salt. Place on greased baking pan and roast for 15 minutes. The underside should be moderately roasted. Turn eggplant and roast for another 5 to 10 minutes till the other side is lightly roasted. Remove from the oven and let cool.

3   Remove the skin from the eggplant and discard. Place the roasted flesh in a large bowl and mash with a fork.

4   Add the Canna-Tahini, garlic, lemon juice, lemon zest, and cumin. Salt to taste, sprinkle with parsley, and serve with your favorite bread or chips.

Approximate dose per serving is based on infusing 5 grams of cured/dried/decarbed cannabis into 5 ounces of oil.

SERVINGS
8
3-ounce
(6-tablespoon)
servings

PREP TIME
40
minutes

COOK TIME
25
minutes

APPROXIMATE THC PER SERVING*
10%: 3.8 mg
15%: 5.7 mg
20%: 7.6 mg

"GREEN" BEAN DIP

This is the ultimate munchie dip, and it pairs well with tortilla chips and Doritos. (Yes, I said it—Doritos! Because every cannabis cookbook should have at least one mention of our favorite party snack.)

Extra-virgin olive oil, for sautéing

½ cup onion, diced

½ cup red pepper, diced

1 jalapeño pepper, seeded and diced (save a few seeds for more spice)

1 (15-ounce) can black beans

2 bay leaves

1 sprig cilantro, leaves chopped

2 tablespoons canna-olive oil, plus 2 tablespoons light olive oil

¼ teaspoon cumin

Salt

1   Heat frying pan for 1 minute. You want your pan to be hot before you add the oil. Add enough olive oil to cover the bottom of the pan.

2   Add onion, red pepper, and jalapeño and sauté for 4 to 6 minutes until onion is golden brown. Drain the excess oil. Add the beans, then mix in the bay leaves, cilantro, and canna-olive oil mixture. Stir.

3   Add the cumin, and salt to taste. Reduce to low heat and simmer for 30 minutes.

4   Remove from heat and scrape into a small bowl. Refrigerate for 30 minutes.

5   Place the bean mixture in a food processor or small blender and pulse until it reaches the desired consistency.

Approximate dose per serving is based on infusing 5 grams of cured/dried/decarbed cannabis into 5 ounces of oil.

SERVINGS
16

PREP TIME
1
hour

COOK TIME
30
minutes

APPROXIMATE THC PER SERVING*

10%:	3.8 mg
15%:	5.7 mg
20%:	7.6 mg

CANNA-COWBOY SALSA

This is yet another delicious chip dip that will have you addicted. The canna-cowboy salsa would be right at home at dinner parties, afternoon snack sessions, tailgates, and football parties. It's best if left to marinate for several hours, so try to make this one the night before if you can.

1 tablespoon canna-olive oil, plus 2 tablespoons light olive oil

¼ cup raw cane sugar

¼ cup cider vinegar

1 (7-ounce) can black beans

1 (7-ounce) can black-eyed peas

1 (15-ounce) can sweet yellow corn

2 plum tomatoes, diced

½ cup onion, diced

½ cup red pepper, diced

½ to 1 habanero pepper, diced (depending on how spicy you want it)

½ cup cilantro, chopped

1   In a small saucepan, combine the canna-olive oil mixture, sugar, and vinegar. Mix over low heat until combined and smooth. Do not boil. Remove from flame and let cool to room temperature, 20 to 30 minutes.

2   In a large bowl, mix together the beans, black-eyed peas, corn, tomatoes, onion, peppers, and cilantro. Add the vinegar mixture to the bean mixture. Cover and refrigerate overnight.

3   Toss, then drain half of the liquid before serving.

Approximate dose per serving is based on infusing 5 grams of cured/dried/decarbed cannabis into 5 ounces of oil.

SERVINGS
16
1-tablespoon
servings

PREP TIME
10
minutes plus
overnight
marinating time

COOK TIME
2–3
minutes

APPROXIMATE
THC PER
SERVING*

10%: 1.9 mg

15%: 2.8 mg

20%: 3.8 mg

TOASTED ONION & DILL CANNA-DIP

This dip is great with Lay's Ruffles—or better yet, Jeff's Salt-and-Pepper Canna-Chips (page 67)!

Light olive oil, for sautéing

2 large red onions, sliced thin and halved

1 teaspoon sea salt

½ teaspoon freshly ground black pepper

1 tablespoon canna-butter

1 package (4 ounces) cream cheese, softened

½ cup sour cream

½ cup Garlic-Dill Canna-Aioli (page 52)

Salt and cayenne pepper

1   Heat medium pan for 1 minute. Coat the bottom of the pan with olive oil.

2   Sauté the onions with salt and black pepper until translucent (5 to 7 minutes). Drain the oil and add the canna-butter to the onions. Continue to sauté on low for 2 to 3 minutes.

3   In the meantime, mix together the cream cheese, sour cream, and canna-aioli in a large bowl until smooth.

4   Add the sautéed onions, and mix well.

5   Season with salt and cayenne pepper to taste.

Approximate dose per serving is based on infusing 5 grams of cured/dried/decarbed cannabis into 1⅓ sticks of butter.

SERVINGS
12

PREP TIME
10
minutes

COOK TIME
20
minutes

APPROXIMATE THC PER SERVING*

10%: 4.4 mg

15%: 6.6 mg

20%: 8.8 mg

Jeff's Salt-and-Pepper Canna-Chips

SERVINGS

12

APPROXIMATE
THC PER
SERVING*

10%: 5 mg

15%: 7.6 mg

20%: 10 mg

2 tablespoons canna–olive oil, plus 2 tablespoons light olive oil

12 large fingerling potatoes, sliced thin on a mandoline

Maldon sea salt

Crushed black pepper

1   Preheat oven to 340°F.

2   Line 2 large baking pans with parchment paper.

3   In a large bowl, drizzle the canna–olive oil mixture over sliced potatoes and toss.

4   Arrange the potato slices on prepared baking sheets, spacing them ⅛ inch apart. Sprinkle with Maldon sea salt and pepper. Bake for 40 minutes, turning halfway through cooking time.

5   Remove when crisp, sprinkle with more salt and pepper, and serve.

*Approximate dose per serving is based on infusing 5 grams of cured/dried/decarbed cannabis into 5 ounces of oil.

CRAZY QUESO

There is nothing quite like this crazy queso to get the party started—especially before the big game. It's crazy easy and crazy good. Enough said.

½ stick creamy canna-butter

3 tablespoons flour (white or whole wheat)

1 cup milk

1 cup grated yellow sharp cheddar cheese

½ teaspoon garlic powder

1 teaspoon onion powder

½ teaspoon cumin

¼ cup diced jalapeño pepper

¼ cup diced tomato

Salt and freshly ground black pepper

1 Melt the canna-butter in a medium saucepan on low heat.

2 Add the flour, 1 tablespoon at a time, and mix to create a paste. Slowly add the milk and stir. Continue to stir and add the cheese, a little at a time. Stir until smooth and creamy. Season with garlic powder, onion powder, and cumin.

3 Remove from the heat and mix in jalapeño pepper and tomato. Add salt and black pepper to taste. Let cool to room temperature, and serve.

Approximate dose per serving is based on infusing 5 grams of cured/dried/decarbed cannabis into 1⅓ sticks of butter.

SERVINGS

12

PREP TIME

10

minutes

COOK TIME

20

minutes

APPROXIMATE THC PER SERVING*

10%: 3.8 mg

15%: 5.7 mg

20%: 7.6 mg

Crazy Chicken Nachos

Pour a batch of crazy queso over a tray full of tortilla chips covered with my "Green" Bean Dip (page 63), jalapeños, and sliced grilled chicken and you've got crazy awesome chicken nachos.

"GREEN" GUACAMOLE

SERVINGS
12

PREP TIME
20
minutes plus
overnight
marinating time

APPROXIMATE
THC PER
SERVING*

10%: 3.8 mg

15%: 5.6 mg

20%: 7.6 mg

Ain't no party like a guacamole party—especially when the canna-oil is infused with a top-shelf sativa strain. Whether it's creamy or chunky, this guacamole is a bright addition to the snack table.

3 avocados, peeled and diced (save the pits)

2 tablespoons canna-olive oil, plus 2 tablespoons light olive oil

2 teaspoons Maldon sea salt

Juice of 1 lime

1 jalapeño, minced

1 garlic clove, minced

1 tablespoon cilantro, minced

½ teaspoon cumin

½ teaspoon cayenne pepper

2 plum tomatoes, diced

¼ onion, diced

Sweet paprika

1   Place the diced avocados in a large bowl and coat with the canna-olive oil mixture and salt. Include the pits in a bowl with the avocados (to keep the avocados from turning brown), cover, and refrigerate overnight.

2   Drain the avocados and mash. Add the lime juice, jalapeño, garlic, and cilantro and mix thoroughly. Add the cumin and cayenne pepper. Carefully fold in the tomatoes and onion.

3   Place a pit in the center of the guacamole, then cover the bowl with plastic wrap and refrigerate for at least 1 hour.

4   Remove from the refrigerator and transfer the guacamole to a serving bowl. Sprinkle with sweet paprika and serve.

Approximate dose per serving is based on infusing 5 grams of cured/dried/decarbed cannabis into 5 ounces of oil.

Wake & Bake Berry Muffins, page 91

CHAPTER NO. 3

Breakfast & Brunch

"REAL" HASH BROWNS

Hash browns may seem simple, but getting them just right can be trickier than you think. I broke down this recipe into many simple steps, and I think you'll agree that the end product is the real deal.

5 Yukon Gold potatoes (1½ to 2 pounds), peeled

½ white onion, grated

2 chives, green part only, chopped

1 medium shallot, grated

¼ cup your favorite cheese, grated

Salt and freshly ground black pepper

2 tablespoons grass-fed butter

2 tablespoons creamy canna-butter, melted

1   Grate the potatoes and onion into a large bowl. Use a ricer to squeeze out as much moisture from the grated potato mixture as possible. If you don't have a ricer, you can transfer the mixture into a cloth towel to twist and squeeze out the moisture.

2   Place the potato mixture in a medium mixing bowl. Add chives, shallot, and cheese.

3   Season with salt and pepper and mix.

4   Melt 1 tablespoon of grass-fed butter in a 10-inch nonstick skillet over medium heat. When the butter melts and starts to foam, add the potato mixture. Evenly distribute the potatoes and press firmly into the bottom of the pan. Reduce heat to low and let the potatoes brown and crisp for 7 minutes.

5   Place a large dinner plate over hash browns. Carefully invert the hash browns onto plate.

6   Add the remaining 1 tablespoon of grass-fed butter to the pan. When the butter melts and starts to foam, slide the hash browns back into the pan. Cook this side over medium heat for 6 to 8 minutes longer. Remove the pan from the heat and evenly drizzle the melted canna-butter onto the hash browns. Let rest for 2 minutes in the pan to allow the canna-butter to seep and infuse into the potatoes.

7   Slide onto a plate or cutting board. Slice into 4 equal pieces and serve warm.

SERVINGS

4

PREP TIME

30

minutes

COOK TIME

20–30

minutes

APPROXIMATE THC PER SERVING*

10%: 5.75 mg

15%: 8.6 mg

20%: 11.5 mg

*Approximate dose per serving is based on infusing 5 grams of cured/dried/decarbed cannabis into 1⅓ sticks of butter.

BLUEBERRY CANNA-COCONUT WAFFLES

Nothing says "wake and bake" like these blueberry coconut waffles, which are a great way to start the day even without the canna-oil. Breakfast in bed, anyone?

1 cup all-purpose flour

1 cup buckwheat flour

1 teaspoon baking powder

1 teaspoon baking soda

1 teaspoon salt

2 teaspoons raw cane sugar

2 eggs

1 cup buttermilk

1 tablespoon extra-virgin canna–coconut oil, melted, plus 3 tablespoons extra-virgin coconut oil, melted

1½ tablespoons shredded coconut, plus more for garnish

¾ cup fresh blueberries

¼ cup Blazed Pecans, slightly crushed (see sidebar, opposite page)

Cooking spray

1   Mix the flours, baking powder, baking soda, salt, and sugar in a large mixing bowl.

2   In a separate bowl, whisk together the eggs, buttermilk, and melted coconut oils.

3   Mix together egg and flour mixtures. Gently fold in the shredded coconut, blueberries, and pecans. Transfer the batter to a large measuring cup to make it easier to pour and measure.

4   Spray waffle iron with nonstick cooking spray.

5   Pour approximately 1 cup of batter onto a preheated waffle iron. Cook until steaming stops (1 to 3 minutes) and waffles are nicely browned and crisp.

6   Garnish with shredded sweet coconut. Serve immediately with Honey-Whipped Canna-Butter (page 49) and maple syrup for a delicious start to your day.

Approximate dose per serving is based on infusing 5 grams of cured/dried/decarbed cannabis into 5 ounces of oil.

SERVINGS

4

waffles

PREP TIME

20

minutes

COOK TIME

1–3

minutes per waffle (depending on your waffle iron)

APPROXIMATE THC PER SERVING (WITHOUT BLAZED PECANS)*

10%:	7.6 mg
15%:	11.4 mg
20%:	15.2 mg

NOTE

If you garnish with Honey—Whipped Canna—Butter (page 49), add the appropriate milligrams per serving.

Blazed Pecans

4 cups pecan halves

¼ cup creamy canna-
butter, melted

½ cup raw cane sugar,
processed "fine"

1 teaspoon cinnamon

1   Preheat oven to 300°F.

2   In a large bowl, mix together the pecans
with the canna-butter and coat evenly. Spread
on a parchment paper–lined cookie sheet. Bake
for 15 minutes.

3   In a small bowl, mix together the sugar and
cinnamon.

4   Remove the pecans from oven. While
they're still hot, sprinkle them with cinnamon-
sugar mixture and toss. Let cool for 30 minutes
before serving.

*Approximate dose per serving is based on infusing 5 grams
of cured/dried/decarbed cannabis into 1⅓ sticks of butter.*

SERVINGS

8

½-cup servings

PREP TIME

5

minutes

COOK TIME

15

minutes

APPROXIMATE
THC PER
SERVING*

10%: 5.6 mg

15%: 8.6 mg

20%: 11.2 mg

PUMPKIN CHOCOLATE-CHIP BLAZED-PECAN MUFFINS

Pumpkin and chocolate chips always make for a winning combination, but the unexpected touch of ginger in these muffins combines with the various spices to create a delectable start to your day. (Just make sure you use a sativa strain!)

SERVINGS
24
muffins

PREP TIME
20
minutes

COOK TIME
30–35
minutes

APPROXIMATE THC PER SERVING*

10%: 5.4 mg

15%: 8.3 mg

20%: 10.9 mg

1 small fresh pumpkin (or one 15-ounce can pumpkin purée)

2 eggs, slightly beaten

¼ cup canna–coconut oil plus ¼ cup extra-virgin coconut oil

½ cup seltzer or soda water

1 teaspoon vanilla extract

½ teaspoon fresh ginger, grated

1½ cups raw cane sugar

1 cup all-purpose flour

¾ cup whole-wheat flour

1 teaspoon baking soda

¼ teaspoon baking powder

¼ teaspoon salt

1 teaspoon cinnamon

½ teaspoon nutmeg

Pinch of ground cloves

½ cup dark chocolate chips

1 cup Blazed Pecans (page 78)

1   Preheat oven to 340°F. Grease two standard-sized muffin tins or line them with paper muffin cups.

2   If using fresh pumpkin, cut, clean, and seed the pumpkin. Leaving the skin on, cut the flesh of the pumpkin into equal-sized chunks about the size of your palm. Boil pumpkin chunks in salted water for 25 minutes. Strain and let cool. Peel skin off and place pumpkin chunks in large bowl. Mash with potato masher or puree in a food processor.

3   Add the eggs, canna–coconut oil mixture, seltzer or soda water, vanilla, fresh ginger, and sugar and mix well.

4   In a separate bowl, sift together flours, baking soda, baking powder, salt, cinnamon, nutmeg, and ground cloves.

5   Combine the dry ingredients with the wet ingredients. Gently fold in the chocolate chips and pecans. Fill the muffin tins three-quarters full. Bake 30 to 35 minutes until tops are lightly golden.

6   Let cool and serve.

Approximate dose per serving is based on infusing 5 grams of cured/dried/decarbed cannabis into 5 ounces of oil.

CANNA-CRAZY OMELET

SERVINGS

2

PREP TIME

15

minutes

COOK TIME

4–6

minutes

APPROXIMATE
THC PER
SERVING*

10%: 3.8 mg

15%: 5.9 mg

20%: 7.5 mg

You haven't had an omelet until you've had this canna-crazy omelet, which is packed with zesty flavor, lots of color, and the right amount of medicine to get your day off to a great start. I suggest you save this for the weekend so you can really enjoy it.

4 eggs

4 teaspoons water

2 teaspoons salt

Freshly ground black pepper

1 teaspoon light olive oil

2 teaspoons grass-fed butter (unsalted)

4 tablespoons shallots, sliced thin

4 small-to-medium mushrooms, sliced thin

½ cup red pepper, diced

¼ cup green pepper, diced

1 teaspoon fresh thyme

Small handful of arugula

2 teaspoons creamy canna-butter, melted

1 tablespoon chives

2 slices Swiss cheese, torn

1   Whisk together the eggs, water, and salt and pepper to taste, and set aside.

2   Heat a 10-inch skillet over medium heat.

3   Place the olive oil and grass-fed butter in the pan. Gently shake and turn the pan to coat the bottom and lower portion of the sides of the pan.

4   When the butter begins to foam, add the shallots and sauté for 3 to 4 minutes. Add the mushrooms, red and green peppers, and thyme. Sauté for 2 to 3 more minutes until the shallots are slightly browned.

5   Add the arugula to the egg mixture. Pour the arugula-egg mixture into the pan.

6   Divide omelet batter into 2 portions, and follow recipe to make 2 separate omelets.

7   Sprinkle the creamy canna-butter on top of the eggs as they are setting. Add the chives and Swiss cheese. Let the mixture cook for 2 to 3 minutes, until the eggs are set (not runny on top). Flip one half over the other.

8   Slide onto a serving plate and serve warm.

*Approximate dose per serving is based on infusing 5 grams of cured/dried/decarbed cannabis into 1⅓ sticks of butter.

CHOCOLATE-CHIP BLAZED-WALNUT CANNA-PANCAKES

My canna-pancakes are big, fluffy, sweet, and satisfying—a Sunday morning treat for sure.

2 cups all-purpose flour, sifted

2 teaspoons baking powder

1 teaspoon salt

1 teaspoon cinnamon

2 tablespoons creamy canna-butter, melted, plus ¼ stick grass-fed butter, melted

1½ cups buttermilk, warm

2 eggs

1 teaspoon vanilla extract

1½ tablespoons cane sugar

1 cup chocolate chips

½ cup blazed walnuts (follow directions for Blazed Pecans, page 78)

Cooking spray

1 Preheat griddle until a drop of water sizzles when it hits the hot surface. Now lower the temperature slightly.

2 Mix together the flour, baking powder, salt, and cinnamon, and set aside.

3 Blend canna-butter mixture, buttermilk, eggs, vanilla, and sugar in a large bowl until smooth.

4 Add the flour mixture and stir until smooth. Mix in the chocolate chips and walnuts. Let the batter rest for 5 minutes.

5 Spray the griddle. Pour 6-inch circles of the batter onto the griddle. Cook for 1 to 2 minutes or until bubbles in batter appear (it's okay to slightly lift the pancake to check browning on the bottom). Flip pancakes and cook an additional 1 minute.

6 Serve with maple syrup and shaved chocolate to complete the decadence.

Approximate dose per serving is based on infusing 5 grams of cured/dried/decarbed cannabis into 1⅓ sticks of butter.

SERVINGS

8

pancakes

PREP TIME

15

minutes

COOK TIME

2–3

minutes per pancake

APPROXIMATE THC PER SERVING*

10%: 3.5 mg

15%: 5.3 mg

20%: 7 mg

EGGS CANNA-DICT WITH CANDIED PEPPER BACON

This recipe is an homage to Julia Child and is by far my favorite wake-and-bake Sunday breakfast. There is just something about this dish that keeps a smile on my face all day long, and it always makes for a nice breakfast-in-bed surprise for that special someone. For perfect poached eggs, pay special attention to Julia's trick of poking the shell of each egg with a pin and placing the eggs in boiling water for 10 seconds before poaching.

SERVINGS

2

PREP TIME

25

minutes

COOK TIME

45

minutes

APPROXIMATE THC PER SERVING*

10%: 5.75 mg

15%: 8.5 mg

20%: 11.5 mg

FOR THE CANDIED PEPPER BACON

¼ cup brown sugar

1 tablespoon maple syrup

8 strips thick-cut bacon or turkey bacon

1 tablespoon crushed black pepper

FOR THE HOLLANDAISE SAUCE

1 tablespoon creamy canna-butter, melted, plus ⅓ cup grass-fed butter, melted

2 egg yolks

1 tablespoons lemon juice

¾ tablespoon lime juice

Pinch of cayenne pepper

⅛ teaspoon Worcestershire sauce

½ tablespoon water

¼ teaspoon salt

PREPARE THE CANDIED BACON

1   Preheat oven to 350ºF.

2   Mix the brown sugar and maple syrup. (For "cherry" bacon, use dark cherry syrup instead of maple syrup.) Coat the bacon with brown sugar–maple syrup mixture, reserving some of this mixture for basting. Place the bacon on a cookie sheet lined with parchment paper, and sprinkle with crushed black pepper.

3   Bake for 35 to 40 minutes. Turn every 10 to 15 minutes, brushing bacon each time with remaining sugar–maple syrup mixture.

PREPARE THE HOLLANDAISE SAUCE

4   Mix the canna-butter with the grass-fed butter and set aside.

5   Fill the bottom of a large pot or double boiler partway with water. Bring water to a gentle simmer. Place glass or metal mixing bowl (or the top of the double boiler) over hot water. The bottom of the bowl should not touch the water.

recipe continues

4 eggs

1 teaspoon distilled white
    vinegar

2 English muffins, split

2 tablespoons grass-fed
    butter, softened

Chopped chives, for
    garnish

6   Whisk the egg yolks into the upper bowl and slowly add lemon and lime juices, cayenne pepper, Worcestershire sauce, and ½ tablespoon of water.

7   Slowly drizzle the melted butters into the egg yolk mixture while whisking. If the sauce begins to get too thick, add another 1 teaspoon of hot water. Continue whisking until all butter is incorporated. Whisk in salt, remove from heat, and cover to keep warm.

POACH THE EGGS

8   Fill a large saucepan halfway with water. Bring water to a boil. Gently poke a small hole in the top of each egg with a pin and boil for 10 seconds. Remove with a slotted spoon, add vinegar to the water, and bring to a simmer.

9   Carefully break each egg into a small glass bowl. This will ensure your yolk has not broken.

10   Using a cooking spoon, gently lower each egg into the simmering water, and cook for 4 minutes. The yolks should still be soft in the center. Remove eggs from water with a slotted spoon and set on large plate lined with a paper towel.

TO FINISH

11   Toast the English muffins and spread with softened butter. Add 2 slices of bacon to each muffin half, followed by 1 poached egg. Gently cover with hollandaise sauce. Sprinkle with chopped chives and serve immediately.

*Approximate dose per serving is based on infusing 5 grams of cured/dried/decarbed cannabis into 1⅓ sticks of butter.

CANNA-COCONUT LIME SMOOTHIES

SERVINGS

2

8-ounce servings

PREP TIME

10

minutes

APPROXIMATE
THC PER
SERVING*

10%: 3.8 mg

15%: 5.9 mg

20%: 7.5 mg

I had my first coconut lime smoothie at a small restaurant while visiting Ecuador several years ago, and I fell in love. It took me a while, but I was finally able to replicate it and make it just a little more "refreshing." Be careful, though–it tastes so good and goes down so smoothly, it'll knock your socks off.

10 ounces coconut milk

½ cup vanilla yogurt

4 teaspoons agave nectar, or 2 teaspoons honey

Juice of 1 lime

1 teaspoon extra-virgin canna–coconut oil

2 tablespoons shredded coconut (sweetened or unsweetened, your preference)

¾ cup ice

1   Place all ingredients into a blender, making sure to place ice on top.

2   Blend for 10 minutes and serve cold.

Approximate dose per serving is based on infusing 5 grams of cured/dried/decarbed cannabis into 5 ounces of oil.

TORTILLA DE PATATAS WITH MUSHROOMS & TARRAGON

The flavors of this non-traditional breakfast tortilla complement the slight herbaceous notes of the cannabis. The mushrooms and tarragon make for delicious additions to the otherwise traditional tortilla. Note: The size of the skillet you use will determine how thin or thick the tortilla is. If you prefer to make a thicker, fluffier tortilla, use an 8- or 10-inch skillet. For a thinner tortilla, use a 12-inch skillet.

5 eggs

2 teaspoons milk

2 tablespoons canna-butter, melted

½ cup Swiss cheese, shredded

¼ cup chives, chopped (reserve some for garnish)

1 tablespoon tarragon

1 teaspoon salt

Freshly ground black pepper

¼ cup light olive oil

½ Spanish onion, chopped

1 cup cremini mushrooms, sliced

1 garlic clove, minced

1 Yukon Gold potato, peeled, sliced, and lightly sprinkled with salt

1   In a large bowl, whisk eggs, milk, melted canna-butter, cheese, chives, tarragon, salt, and pepper. Set aside.

2   Preheat a medium- or large-sized (see headnote), seasoned cast-iron skillet for 1 to 2 minutes. Add enough oil to cover the bottom of the skillet. Add the onion and sauté for 3 to 5 minutes until translucent. Add the mushrooms and sauté until they release liquid, about 5 minutes. Add the garlic and continue to sauté for 2 minutes. Remove the mixture to a plate while you cook your potatoes.

3   Cook the potato in your now-empty pan, being careful to keep the slices separated so they don't stick to one another. Turn after 3 minutes. Transfer potato to a plate and let cool for 10 minutes.

4   Pour the remaining oil into the skillet, and reheat on high for 2 minutes.

5   Meanwhile, add the potato and mushrooms to the egg mixture, and pour back into the pan. Immediately lower the heat to medium.

6   Gently shake the pan and cook until the sides of the tortilla are set and the center is starting to set.

7   Carefully slide the tortilla onto a plate with the cooked side down. It's best to do this over a sink, being cautious so as not to spill any hot oil onto yourself or other surfaces.

8   Add more oil if necessary to coat the bottom and sides of the pan and reheat over medium heat.

9   Flip the tortilla back into the pan, uncooked side down, and cook until set, 4 to 5 minutes. Gently shake and use a spatula if necessary to ensure the tortilla doesn't stick. Invert from the pan onto a plate, and sprinkle with reserved chives.

10   Cut into 8 wedges and serve.

Approximate dose per serving is based on infusing 5 grams of cured/dried/decarbed cannabis into 1⅓ sticks of butter.

WAKE & BAKE BERRY MUFFINS

These berry muffins are moist and delicious and serve as the perfect contribution to any brunch gathering.

SERVINGS

12

muffins

PREP TIME

15

minutes

COOK TIME

25

minutes

APPROXIMATE
THC PER
SERVING*

10%: 3.8 mg

15%: 5.7 mg

20%: 7.6 mg

FOR THE MUFFIN BATTER

1 cup whole-wheat flour

1 cup all-purpose flour, plus 1 tablespoon

2 teaspoons baking powder

½ teaspoon sea salt

1 teaspoon confectioners' sugar

½ cup fresh blueberries

½ cup fresh strawberries

½ cup fresh blackberries or raspberries

½ stick creamy canna-butter, softened, plus ½ stick grass-fed butter, softened

¾ cup raw cane sugar

2 eggs

1 teaspoon almond extract

¼ teaspoon lime zest

½ cup whole milk

1   Preheat oven to 340°F.

2   Line muffin tin with paper muffin cups.

3   Sift 1 cup all-purpose flour, 1 cup whole-wheat flour, baking powder, and salt into a large bowl.

4   In a small bowl, mix together the remaining 1 tablespoon of all-purpose flour with the confectioners' sugar. Place berries in a separate bowl. Sprinkle and coat with the flour–confectioners' sugar mixture.

5   In another bowl, cream the canna-butter mixture with cane sugar until smooth. Mix in eggs, almond extract, and lime zest.

6   Slowly fold in the flours, baking powder, and salt mixture while adding the milk. Gently add the berries to the batter. Do not overmix or you will end up smashing the berries.

7   Carefully spoon the batter into muffin cups. Each muffin cup should be three-quarters full.

recipe continues

FOR THE CRUMB TOPPING

1 tablespoon whole-wheat flour

1 tablespoon all-purpose flour

¼ stick grass-fed butter, diced

4 tablespoons raw cane sugar

1 or 2 pinches of cinnamon

8   Make the crumb topping by combining all the crumb-topping ingredients in a medium bowl. Using two knives or a fork, cut the grass-fed butter with the dry ingredients to create "crumbles." Sprinkle on top of batter in the muffin cups.

9   Bake for 25 to 30 minutes, until a toothpick inserted into the center comes out clean.

10   Let cool and serve.

Approximate dose per serving is based on infusing 5 grams of cured/dried/decarbed cannabis into 1⅓ sticks of butter.

PEPPERED AVOCADO & EGG WHITES WITH SPINACH ON CANNA-BUTTERED FRENCH BREAD CROSTINI

This is one of my favorite early-morning recipes. It's a fun, simple, and super-healthy breakfast to get you going any day of the week.

SERVINGS
4

PREP TIME
15
minutes

COOK TIME
10
minutes

APPROXIMATE THC PER SERVING*

10%:	3.8 mg
15%:	5.9 mg
20%:	7.6 mg

2 ripe avocados

Maldon sea salt

Whites of 8 large eggs

8 slices French bread

8 teaspoons creamy canna-butter

¼ cup baby spinach, uncooked

Grass-fed butter or oil, for the skillet

Crushed black pepper

½ teaspoon red pepper flakes

1   Halve and pit the avocados. Cut the avocado halves into quarters. Set them aside in a bowl with the pits (to keep the avocado from turning brown). Sprinkle the avocado quarters with Maldon sea salt.

2   Separate the egg whites from the yolks, keeping each egg white separate and reserving the yolks for another use.

3   Toast the French bread and butter each slice with 1 teaspoon of creamy canna-butter. Place 1 or 2 spinach leaves on top of each piece of buttered toast.

4   In a lightly oiled skillet, fry each egg white until firm. Flip and fry the other side for 10 to 15 seconds. Season with Maldon sea salt and black pepper to taste. Place an egg on top of the spinach on each slice of toast.

5   With a fork, lightly press each quartered avocado so that it is somewhat flat. Place a flattened quarter on top of the egg and sprinkle liberally with black pepper, red pepper flakes, and a bit more Maldon sea salt before serving.

Approximate dose per serving is based on infusing 5 grams of cured/dried/decarbed cannabis into 5 ounces of oil.

CANNA-BANANA BREAD WITH BLAZED PECANS

I find that most banana breads tend to be rather dry, but this recipe produces a seriously tasty, moist, and medicinally powerful banana bread. And who doesn't like saying "canna-banana"?

Cooking spray or oil to grease pan

1½ cups all-purpose flour

1 teaspoon baking soda

½ teaspoon salt

¼ cup creamy canna-butter, softened (or canna–coconut oil), plus ¼ cup grass-fed butter, softened (or extra-virgin coconut oil)

1 cup raw cane sugar

½ teaspoon vanilla

2 eggs, beaten

4 ripe bananas, mashed

1 cup Blazed Pecans (page 78)

1   Preheat oven to 340°F. Grease and lightly flour a 9-by-5-inch loaf pan.

2   In a small bowl, sift together flour, baking soda, and salt. Set aside.

3   In a large bowl, cream the canna-butter mixture, sugar, vanilla, and eggs with a wooden spoon until fluffy. Add in the mashed bananas and pecans. Stir in the dry ingredients.

4   Pour the batter into the prepared pan and bake for 1 hour, or until a toothpick inserted into center comes out clean. This may take an extra 10 minutes or so.

5   Remove the banana bread from the oven and let cool for 30 minutes, then turn the pan onto a wire rack to release. Serve and enjoy!

Approximate dose per serving is based on infusing 5 grams of cured/dried/decarbed cannabis into 1⅓ sticks of butter.

SERVINGS
10

PREP TIME
15
minutes

COOK TIME
1
hour

APPROXIMATE THC PER SERVING*

10%: 5.7 mg

15%: 8.6 mg

20%: 11.4 mg

Hazy Thai Wings, page 115

PEASANT BREAD GRILLED CHEESE

The secret to this recipe is to spread the canna-butter on the inside of each slice of bread to keep it at a cooler temperature so it doesn't lose its potency. Otherwise, it's hard to go wrong with toasted, buttery bread that's oozing with melted cheese—you have my guarantee that, once served, these won't last long!

SERVINGS
4

PREP TIME
10
minutes

COOK TIME
20
minutes

APPROXIMATE THC PER SERVING*

10%: 3.8 mg

15%: 5.7 mg

20%: 7.6 mg

8 slices peasant bread, or 4 peasant bread rolls, split

4 tablespoons grass-fed butter, softened

4 teaspoons creamy canna-butter, softened

Dijon mustard

2 Roma tomatoes, sliced thinly lengthwise into eighths

8 slices Havarti cheese

8 slices Swiss cheese

1   Preheat oven to 340°F.

2   Butter one side of each slice of bread with grass-fed butter and place butter side down on a cookie sheet.

3   Butter the face-up side of 4 slices of bread with creamy canna-butter.

4   Spread the Dijon mustard on the face-up side of the remaining 4 slices of bread.

5   Position 2 tomato slices on top of the Dijon mustard.

6   Layer the cheeses on top of the tomato slices.

7   Place the canna-buttered bread on top of the cheese, facedown (regular butter should be on the outside).

8   Slide the cookie sheet into the oven and bake for 10 minutes.

9   Using a spatula, press down on each sandwich to flatten a bit, then turn each sandwich over and bake for an additional 10 minutes, until toasted and golden brown.

Approximate dose per serving is based on infusing 5 grams of cured/dried/decarbed cannabis into 1⅓ sticks of butter.

POTATO LATKES WITH CANNA-PEAR CRÈME FRAÎCHE

This fun recipe was inspired by my friend Chef Eric Greenspan's Latke Bites with Apple Crème Fraîche, which is one of my favorite non-infused snacks. Although my recipe is quite different from his, his concept of fruit-infused crème fraîche is a wonderful contemporary take on the old-world culinary staple of latkes with applesauce. To make your own crème fraîche, just mix 1 cup whipping cream with 2 tablespoons buttermilk in a glass container. Cover with a tight-fitting lid and let stand at room temperature until very thick (8 to 24 hours). Stir well and then refrigerate. Will keep refrigerated for up to 10 days.

SERVINGS
18–24
depending on size

PREP TIME
40
minutes

COOK TIME
12–14
minutes per batch
of pancakes

APPROXIMATE
THC PER
SERVING*

10%:
1.9–2.5 mg

15%:
2.8–3.8 mg

20%:
3.8–5.1 mg

FOR THE PEAR CRÈME FRAÎCHE

Juice of 1 lemon

2 Anjou or Bartlett pears, peeled, sliced, and cored

4 teaspoons raw cane sugar

4 teaspoons brown sugar

2 tablespoons canna-butter, plus 2 tablespoons grass-fed butter

Cornstarch slurry (1 teaspoon cornstarch mixed with 1 teaspoon water)

Dash of cinnamon

1 cup crème fraîche

MAKE THE PEAR CRÈME FRAÎCHE

1   Sprinkle lemon juice over pears.

2   Melt the cane sugar, brown sugar, and canna-butter mixture in a nonstick skillet over low heat, stirring occasionally, until smooth, about 5 minutes. Turn the heat up to medium-low and add the pears. Cook, gently stirring every 5 to 6 minutes, until pears are tender. Add the cornstarch slurry and cinnamon and cook 1 to 2 minutes until thickened. Remove from the heat. Drain the syrup and set aside to let cool for 15 minutes.

3   Add 2 tablespoons of the cooled pear sauce to the crème fraîche and whisk until incorporated. Refrigerate while making the potato latkes.

recipe continues

6 medium Idaho or russet
    potatoes

1 small onion

2 eggs, slightly beaten

2 tablespoons flour

½ teaspoon salt

Dash of freshly ground
    black pepper

1 teaspoon tarragon,
    chopped

1 teaspoon chives, minced

½ teaspoon baking
    powder

Light coconut oil or olive
    oil for frying

MAKE THE LATKES

4   Peel the potatoes and onion and grate into a large colander or strainer.

5   Squeeze out as much water as possible from the potatoes and onion and transfer them to a large bowl. Stir in the eggs. Add the flour, salt, pepper, tarragon, chives, and baking powder, and mix.

6   Preheat a large frying pan for 1 minute. Add coconut or olive oil and reduce heat to medium.

7   Using a spoon, drop about ¼-cup dollops of the potato mixture into the pan, flatten, and fry for 6 to 7 minutes on each side until golden brown. Remove with a slotted spatula and drain on a plate lined with paper towels or brown paper.

8   Serve with pear crème fraîche, garnished with candied pears and drizzled with remaining pear sauce.

Approximate dose per serving is based on infusing 5 grams of cured/dried/decarbed cannabis into 5 ounces of oil.

BUFFALO CHICKEN POPPERS

Poppin' with flavor, these were my kids' favorite Saturday-afternoon snack before I started cooking with cannabis. Now they're all grown up—and so is my recipe!

1 cup flour

2 teaspoons salt

1 teaspoon baking powder

1 teaspoon garlic powder

1 teaspoon onion powder

4 large eggs

1 cup breadcrumbs

2 teaspoons Old Bay seasoning

6 boneless chicken cutlets, pounded flat and cut into 1-inch bite-size pieces

Olive oil for frying

2 tablespoons canna–olive oil, plus 2 tablespoons light olive oil

Frank's Buffalo Wing Sauce (or your favorite buffalo wing sauce)

1   Line up three medium bowls.

2   In the first bowl, sift together flour, 1 teaspoon salt, baking powder, garlic, and onion powder.

3   In the second bowl, beat the eggs.

4   In the third bowl, combine breadcrumbs and Old Bay seasoning.

5   Place the chicken pieces in the first bowl and coat with flour mixture.

6   Dunk each "floured" chicken piece into the egg and then put it into the breadcrumb mixture to coat.

7   Preheat a large frying pan on high for 1 minute.

8   Add enough olive oil to fill ½ inch from bottom. Reduce the heat to medium. (Make sure frying pan handle is pointed away from you.) Carefully place the coated chicken pieces in the pan. Make sure they are spaced and not overlapping. Fry for 5 to 7 minutes until golden brown. You might have to do this in batches. Remove from the heat, place on brown paper or a paper towel, and drizzle with canna–olive oil mixture.

9   Sprinkle with more Old Bay, smother with Frank's Buffalo Wing Sauce or your favorite wing sauce, and serve (with plenty of napkins!).

SERVINGS
8
(approximately 8 pieces per serving)

PREP TIME
20
minutes

COOK TIME
5–7
minutes per batch

APPROXIMATE THC PER SERVING*

10%:	7.6 mg
15%:	11.4 mg
20%:	15.2 mg

*Approximate dose per serving is based on infusing 5 grams of cured/dried/decarbed cannabis into 5 ounces of oil.

SPINACH & FETA CANNA-BOREKAS

With flaky dough and a flavorful filling, borekas can't be beat. You'll be licking your fingers—and reaching for another one.

SERVINGS
12
large borekas

PREP TIME
20
minutes

COOK TIME
30
minutes

APPROXIMATE THC PER SERVING*

10%: 3.8 mg

15%: 5.6 mg

20%: 7.6 mg

FOR THE FILLING

2 tablespoons olive oil

½ cup onion, diced

1 pound fresh spinach

Sea salt and freshly ground black pepper

¼ cup crumbled feta cheese

½ cup grated Swiss cheese

1 large egg, lightly beaten

¼ cup chopped fresh parsley

1 tablespoon chopped fresh dill

MAKE THE FILLING

1   Preheat a frying pan for 1 minute. Add the olive oil to cover the bottom of the pan.

2   Sauté the onion until translucent. Add spinach and sauté until wilted and cooked. Add salt and pepper to taste. Remove from heat and transfer the mixture to a colander suspended in a large bowl. Let it drain for about 10 minutes and then move to a large bowl. Add feta, Swiss cheese, egg, parsley, and dill. Mix well, and again add salt and pepper to taste.

MAKE THE BOREKAS

3   Preheat oven to 340°F.

4   Use a pastry brush to coat the bottom of a cookie sheet with some of the melted canna-butter mixture.

5   Cut the phyllo dough long ways into 5- or 6-inch strips. Stack them and cover with a towel so they don't dry out.

6   Working one at a time, brush each strip with canna-butter mixture, fold over lengthwise, and butter again.

recipe continues

4 tablespoons creamy
   canna-butter, plus 4
   tablespoons grass-fed
   butter, melted

6 to 8 sheets of phyllo
   dough, thawed

1 large egg

Black or regular sesame
   seeds, for sprinkling

7   Place 1 tablespoon of the filling on the end. Fold up like a flag, bottom edge to side edge, then continue folding until you reach the end of your dough to form a triangle. Butter the outside at the end.

8   Repeat with the remaining filling and dough.

9   Beat the egg and brush the top of each boreka and sprinkle with sesame seeds.

10   Place the borekas on the buttered cookie sheet and bake for 20 to 25 minutes until golden brown. Remove, cool, and serve.

Approximate dose per serving is based on infusing 5 grams of cured/dried/decarbed cannabis into 1⅓ sticks of butter.

MINI RICOTTA PINEAPPLE CANNA-CREPE SOUFFLÉS

One of my all-time favorite dishes! I make 6 minis to snack on during the week. You can also make one large soufflé by placing all the blintzes on top of the melted butter in a large baking dish. Then just pour the soufflé mixture over the crepes and bake for 1 hour.

SERVINGS
6
2-ounce ramekins

PREP TIME
15
minutes

COOK TIME
1
hour

APPROXIMATE THC PER SERVING*

10%:	7.7 mg
15%:	11.5 mg
20%:	15.4 mg

FOR THE CREPES

1 cup milk

¼ cup cold water

1 cup all-purpose flour

1 tablespoon sugar

2 eggs, lightly beaten

¼ cup creamy canna-butter, melted and cooled

1 stick grass-fed butter, cold (you won't use the whole stick—it's just to grease the pan)

FOR THE CHEESE FILLING

1 cup ricotta cheese

½ cup mascarpone cheese

3 tablespoons confectioners' sugar

¼ cup crushed pineapple, drained

1 egg

1   Blend together the crepe ingredients: milk, cold water, flour, sugar, eggs, and canna-butter.

2   Heat a small nonstick pan on medium. Rub the stick of grass-fed butter around bottom and sides of the pan.

3   Pour enough batter into the pan to coat the bottom. Cook for 30 to 40 seconds until the batter sets. Shake gently to loosen. Flip, using a small silicone spatula, and cook another 30 to 40 seconds. Transfer to a plate and repeat until all the batter is used.

4   In a medium mixing bowl, combine cheese-filling ingredients: ricotta cheese, mascarpone cheese, confectioners' sugar, crushed pineapple, and egg. Mix well.

5   Place 1 tablespoon of the cheese filling in each crepe and fold the bottom of the crepe over the filling. Fold in both sides and then roll up over folded edges to create a closed little blintz. Set aside and repeat.

recipe continues

FOR THE SOUFFLÉ

1 stick grass-fed butter, melted

1 cup sugar

4 eggs

1½ cups sour cream

2 teaspoons pineapple juice

2 teaspoons vanilla

Pinch of cinnamon

½ cup crushed pineapple

½ teaspoon salt

6   Preheat oven to 340°F.

7   Pour 1 to 2 tablespoons of melted butter to cover the bottom of each of six 8-ounce ramekins. Place 1 crepe in each ramekin.

8   Blend the remaining soufflé ingredients: sugar, eggs, sour cream, pineapple juice, vanilla, cinnamon, crushed pineapple, and salt. Pour the mixture over the crepes, filling each ramekin three-quarters full. Bake for 1 hour until golden brown and then serve.

Approximate dose per serving is based on infusing 5 grams of cured/dried/decarbed cannabis into 1⅓ sticks of butter.

MAUI ONION POTATO PIEROGI

These delicious dumplings are of Eastern European origin and make for a hearty appetizer. Both the dough and the filling are simple to make, and you can have fun dressing them up with the toppings at the end.

2 cups flour

½ teaspoon salt, plus more to taste

1 egg, lightly beaten

½ cup water, room temperature

2 tablespoons grass-fed butter

¼ cup grated Maui or Vidalia onion

1 clove garlic, pressed

2 tablespoons canna-butter, plus 2 tablespoons grass-fed butter, softened

¼ cup shredded pepper jack cheese

1 cup cold mashed potatoes

Freshly ground black pepper

1   Sift together the flour and ½ teaspoon salt. Add the beaten egg and stir until a shaggy dough starts to form. Add the water a little at a time until the dough comes together. Knead for about 5 minutes until the dough is smooth and pliable. Cover with a towel and let sit for 30 minutes.

2   In the meantime, melt the grass-fed butter in a medium saucepan. Add onion and sauté until golden brown. Add the garlic and continue to sauté for 1 minute. Remove from the heat and add the canna-butter mixture. Mix the onion-butter mixture and cheese into mashed potatoes.

3   Taste to adjust the salt and add freshly ground black pepper to taste.

4   Roll the dough out on a floured surface to ¼-inch thickness.

5   Use a cookie cutter or a drinking glass to cut out circles. Ideally, the circles should be about 3 inches in diameter. You can use the dough scraps to reroll a second time, and possibly a third time if the dough doesn't feel too tough. After that, discard any scraps that remain.

SERVINGS
15
pierogi

PREP TIME
20
minutes

COOK TIME
15
minutes

IDLE TIME
30
minutes

APPROXIMATE THC PER SERVING*

10%: 3.3 mg
15%: 4.8 mg
20%: 6.5 mg

6   Place 1 to 1½ teaspoons of the potato filling on one half of each dough circle. Fold empty half over the filling and crimp edges with fingertips to close. Make sure there are no openings for the filling to seep out. If they are difficult to crimp together, wet the edges with water before folding over.

7   Fill a large pot with salted water. Bring to a rapid boil. Drop pierogi into the rapidly boiling water and boil for 4 to 6 minutes. When they're fully cooked, they'll start to rise to the top of the water. Remove with a slotted spoon.

8   You can serve boiled with sour cream and chives or fry in butter with some onions until golden brown (my favorite).

Approximate dose per serving is based on infusing 5 grams of cured/dried/decarbed cannabis into 1⅓ sticks of butter.

STONED PEPPER PECAN NOODLE PUDDING

This is always a big holiday hit and top request with my family. Both delicately sweet and pungently spicy, the pudding finds a nice balance. Pepper lovers in particular will lap it up.

1 package (12 ounces) thin egg noodles or vermicelli

1 tablespoon canna-butter, melted, plus ¼ cup grass-fed butter, melted

¼ cup coconut oil

¾ cup cane sugar

¾ cup brown sugar

4 large eggs

¾ teaspoon ground white pepper

1 teaspoon freshly ground black pepper

Pinch of cinnamon

1 teaspoon sea salt

½ cup Blazed Pecans (page 78)

1 Preheat oven to 340°F. Grease a 9-by-13-inch pan and set aside.

2 Cook noodles as per the manufacturer's instructions. The pasta should be al dente (cooked yet firm). Rinse in cold water, drain, and drizzle with 1 tablespoon of melted canna-butter mixture. Set aside.

3 In a saucepan, heat the coconut oil and sugars on low until they start to bubble (they will be grainy, but don't worry; they will dissolve when you combine with the noodles). When bubbling, immediately turn off the heat and mix in the remaining canna-butter mixture. Add the noodles and stir until they're evenly coated. Let cool to room temperature.

4 While cooling, beat the eggs, peppers, cinnamon, and salt. Add this mixture to the room-temperature noodle mixture. Toss in the pecans.

5 Pour into the prepared pan and bake at 340°F for 50 minutes.

6 Remove from the oven. If it's not perfectly set, or if you need to make it ahead to eat later, you can cover it and put it in the refrigerator for 1 hour.

7 Serve immediately, or, if you've refrigerated it, rewarm it in the oven for 15 minutes at 300°F.

SERVINGS
10

PREP TIME
20
minutes

COOK TIME
1
hour and 10 minutes

APPROXIMATE THC PER SERVING*

10%: 2.8 mg

15%: 4.2 mg

20%: 5.7 mg

*Approximate dose per serving is based on infusing 5 grams of cured/dried/decarbed cannabis into 1⅓ sticks of butter.

FLYING PIGS IN BLANKETS

This is a classic appetizer that's always a big hit. It's one of my simplest party recipes—and a very tasty one at that! A few of these per person are sure to get things off to a fun start.

SERVINGS

24

(1 pig-in-blanket)
servings

PREP TIME

20

minutes

COOK TIME

15

minutes

APPROXIMATE
THC PER
SERVING*

10%: 1.2 mg

15%: 1.9 mg

20%: 2.5 mg

3 packages refrigerated biscuit dough

1 tablespoon canna-olive oil, plus 3 tablespoons light olive oil

2 tablespoons spicy brown mustard

24 mini hot dogs or 8 hot dogs cut into 24 pieces

1 egg yolk, beaten

1   Separate biscuit dough sections and place on a parchment paper-lined cookie sheet.

2   In a small bowl, whisk together the canna-olive oil mixture and mustard. Brush each biscuit with this mixture.

3   Place 1 hot dog on top of each biscuit and wrap biscuit dough around it. Place it seam side down on baking sheet. Brush the top of each hot dog with egg yolk.

4   Bake for 12 to 15 minutes until biscuits are golden brown, then watch them disappear once you serve them.

Approximate dose per serving is based on infusing 5 grams of cured/dried/decarbed cannabis into 5 ounces of oil.

HAZY THAI WINGS

This recipe is an ode to Pok Pok, Chef Andy Ricker's renowned Thai street-food restaurant. The first time I had authentic Thai wings was at Pok Pok Noi in Portland, while visiting Chef Adrian Hale of *Communal Table*—and I fell in love. For days, all I could think about was how to re-create these awesome wings with one (or two) added ingredients. And here you have it! You'll never look at wings the same way again, guaranteed.

½ cup raw cane sugar

½ cup Asian fish sauce

3 tablespoons ketchup

1½ tablespoons chili garlic sauce (Sambal)

1 tablespoon fresh lime juice

1 teaspoon rice vinegar

1 cup cornstarch

1 teaspoon garlic powder

2 pounds chicken wings, rinsed and patted dry

Extra-virgin coconut oil for frying

1 tablespoon canna-coconut oil, plus 3 tablespoons extra-virgin coconut oil

Toasted Peanuts & Garlic (see sidebar, page 117)

4 tablespoons cilantro, chopped

1   Place sugar in a food processor and grind until very fine.

2   In a medium bowl, combine the fish sauce, ketchup, sugar, chili garlic sauce, lime juice, and rice vinegar. Set aside.

3   In a shallow dish, sift the cornstarch and garlic powder. Toss the wings in the cornstarch mixture to coat.

recipe continues

SERVINGS
4
(4–5 wings per serving)

PREP TIME
30
minutes

COOK TIME
30
minutes

APPROXIMATE THC PER SERVING*
10%: 6.5 mg
15%: 9 mg
20%: 13 mg

4   Heat a large skillet on the stovetop for 1 minute on high. Add enough extra-virgin coconut oil to fry, about 2 inches from the bottom of the pan. Fry the wings until golden brown. Remove with slotted spoon and drain on brown paper.

5   Preheat oven to 340°F.

6   Place the fried wings on a lightly greased baking sheet and drizzle each wing with 1 teaspoon of canna-coconut oil mixture. Bake for 7 to 8 minutes.

7   In a clean skillet, heat the sauce on medium until syrupy, about 5 minutes.

8   Remove the wings from the oven and toss with the sauce until evenly coated. Toss in the peanuts and garlic.

9   Garnish with cilantro and serve alongside a cup of carrot sticks and celery curls.

Approximate dose per serving is based on infusing 5 grams of cured/dried/decarbed cannabis into 5 ounces of oil.

CELERY CURLS

Cut celery into 6-inch pieces, slice in half lengthwise, make lengthwise cuts almost to center and repeat to create slivers. Refrigerate in ice water until slivers curl.

Toasted Peanuts & Garlic

¼ cup raw peanuts, crushed

4 cloves garlic, chopped

1 teaspoon coconut oil

Dash of salt

In a small bowl, mix peanuts and garlic with coconut oil and a dash of salt. Spread evenly on a small pan and roast at 325°F for 30 minutes, until toasted and browned. Remove and let cool.

DEVILED EGGS WITH CANNABIS-INFUSED SHALLOTS & CUCUMBER

Believe it or not, this is a big Mother's Day brunch favorite. In addition to looking scrumptious, the "cannabinized" shallots coupled with the crispy cucumber are the secret—a combination no mother (or pretty much no one else, for that matter) can resist.

SERVINGS

12

deviled-egg halves

PREP TIME

30

minutes

COOK TIME

10

minutes

APPROXIMATE THC PER SERVING*

10%:	2.8 mg
15%:	4.2 mg
20%:	5.6 mg

Approximate dose per serving is based on infusing 5 grams of cured/dried/decarbed cannabis into 1⅓ sticks of butter.

6 eggs

1 shallot, sliced thin or diced small (whatever you prefer)

1 teaspoon light olive oil

1½ tablespoons canna-butter

½ thin leek, sliced thin

2 tablespoons mayonnaise

2 teaspoons Dijon mustard

½ teaspoon salt, plus more to taste

½ Persian or hothouse cucumber, julienned or sliced very thin

Cayenne pepper

1   Boil eggs for 10 minutes until hard-boiled.

2   While eggs are boiling, sauté the shallot in olive oil until translucent and light brown. Remove from the heat and drain oil. Add the canna-butter and leek to the shallot in the warm pan and gently mix to coat. Move the mixture to a cool bowl and set aside.

3   Remove the eggs and place in cold water. Roll each egg on a hard surface to crack its shell, and then peel it under cold water. Cut the eggs in half lengthwise.

4   Remove the yolks and place them in a mixing bowl. Add mayonnaise, mustard, and salt to egg yolks, and whisk until creamy. Mix in the shallot and leek (I like to set some aside to add to the garnish later).

5   Place the egg yolk mixture in a ziplock baggie or pastry-piping bag with a round nozzle. Cut off a ¼-inch tip from one corner of the baggie. Squeeze the egg yolk mixture into the egg white halves.

6   Garnish with cucumber slices, sprinkle with cayenne pepper, and voilà!

Krazy Kale & Hemp Seed Salad with
Curried Orange Dressing, page 130

Soups, Salads & Sides

FIVE-PEPPER BLAZED POTATOES

These five-pepper POTatoes are like a five-alarm fire of deliciousness (not heat)—but you can alter the amount of jalapeño to increase or decrease the level of spice according to taste.

Olive oil, for sautéing

1 large sweet onion, diced

½ teaspoon salt

5 large Idaho potatoes, washed, unpeeled, diced into ½-inch cubes

1 teaspoon coarsely crushed black pepper

¼ cup white wine (I prefer Riesling)

1 red pepper, diced

1 yellow pepper, diced

1 jalapeño pepper, sliced thin

1 tablespoon canna–olive oil, plus 3 tablespoons light olive oil

1 tablespoon grass-fed butter

2 teaspoons chili garlic sauce (also known as Sambal)

Salt

1   Preheat large skillet for 1 minute on high. Add enough olive oil to coat the bottom of pan. Add the onion and salt and sauté until onion is translucent. Add potatoes and black pepper. Continue to sauté for 10 to 12 minutes, stirring occasionally.

2   Pour in the white wine and scrape the bottom of the pan to deglaze the crispy bits that have formed on the bottom. Add the red, yellow, and jalapeño peppers. Cover and cook for 5 to 7 minutes, until all the liquid is absorbed. Lower the heat to a simmer and add the canna–olive oil mixture and grass-fed-butter. Gently mix until potatoes are evenly coated.

3   Add chili garlic sauce and lightly toss. Salt to taste, if necessary.

4   Use a slotted spoon to transfer to a serving dish and serve warm.

Approximate dose per serving is based on infusing 5 grams of cured/dried/decarbed cannabis into 5 ounces of oil.

SERVINGS
8

PREP TIME
20
minutes

COOK TIME
30–40
minutes

APPROXIMATE THC PER SERVING*

10%: 3.5 mg

15%: 5.7 mg

20%: 7 mg

CANNA-BUTTERED GARLIC BROCCOLI & CAULIFLOWER

Like pretty much everyone else, I hated broccoli when I was growing up. But when my first boyfriend introduced me to buttered broccoli with garlic, I was smitten (admittedly, butter and garlic make most things taste pretty great). Here, I've doctored the recipe a bit further for you with some turmeric and lemon.

2 teaspoons olive oil

3 tablespoons grass-fed butter

2 cloves garlic, pressed

1 teaspoon turmeric

2 tablespoons creamy canna-butter

2 cups broccoli florets

2 cups cauliflower florets

2 tablespoons water

¼ cup toasted almond slivers (optional)

1 tablespoon lemon juice

1 teaspoon lemon zest

Maldon sea salt

1   Preheat large saucepot for 1 minute on medium heat.

2   Add the olive oil, grass-fed butter, garlic, and turmeric. Stir to mix well. Add in the canna-butter, melt, and stir. Immediately add the broccoli and cauliflower and stir to coat.

3   Add 2 tablespoons water. Cover and let steam on medium heat for 4 to 5 minutes.

4   Remove from heat; add the slivered almonds (if using), lemon juice, and lemon zest; and stir. Cover for another 2 to 3 minutes to allow all flavors to settle.

5   Transfer to serving dish and flavor to taste with Maldon sea salt before eating.

Approximate dose per serving is based on infusing 5 grams of cured/dried/decarbed cannabis into 1⅓ sticks of butter.

SERVINGS
8

PREP TIME
20
minutes

COOK TIME
5–8
minutes

APPROXIMATE THC PER SERVING*

10%: 2.9 mg

15%: 4.3 mg

20%: 5.8 mg

CANNA-CAESAR SALAD WITH GRILLED CHICKEN

This is a great café-style lunch. The lemon zest makes for a nice touch, especially with the extra herbal flavor of the cannabis-infused dressing.

4 cups romaine lettuce, torn or as chiffonade (see sidebar, page 218)

6 chicken breasts, grilled and cut into 2-inch strips

6 anchovy fillets packed in oil

1 medium garlic clove

Salt

2 large egg yolks

2 tablespoons fresh lemon juice, zest from lemon reserved

¾ teaspoon Dijon mustard

2 tablespoons canna–olive oil, plus ¼ cup extra-virgin olive oil

4 tablespoons finely grated Parmesan

Freshly ground black pepper

2 cups Canna-Croutons (see sidebar, page 126)

1   Place the lettuce in a large bowl. Add the chicken and toss.

2   Chop the anchovies, garlic, and ½ teaspoon salt together, and mash into a paste.

3   Whisk together the egg yolks, lemon juice, and Dijon mustard.

4   Add the anchovy-garlic paste and continue to whisk until thick and smooth. Slowly whisk in the canna–olive oil mixture until the dressing emulsifies and becomes thick. Continue to whisk and slowly add the Parmesan cheese. Add the reserved lemon zest and salt and pepper to taste.

5   Add dressing to lettuce and chicken. Add croutons, toss, and serve.

SERVINGS

12

side salads / 6 entrées

PREP TIME

30

minutes

COOK TIME

15

minutes

APPROXIMATE THC PER SERVING (WITHOUT CANNA-CROUTONS)*

| 10%: 2.5–5 mg |
| 15%: 3.8–7.6 mg |
| 20%: 5–10 mg |

Canna-Croutons

8 pieces of bread (your choice)

1 teaspoon canna-oil

3 tablespoons extra-virgin olive oil

½ teaspoon dried oregano

½ teaspoon dried basil

½ teaspoon dried rosemary

1 teaspoon salt

Tear the bread into 1-inch pieces and put it in a large bowl. Mix together the canna-oil, extra-virgin olive oil, dried oregano, dried basil, dried rosemary, and salt. Coat bread pieces evenly. Place on a baking sheet and bake at 340°F for 20 minutes. Check and toss every few minutes or so.

Approximate dose per serving is based on infusing 5 grams of cured/dried/decarbed cannabis into 5 ounces of oil.

SERVINGS
8

PREP TIME
5
minutes

COOK TIME
20
minutes

APPROXIMATE THC PER SERVING*

10%: 1.3 mg

15%: 1.9 mg

20%: 2.6 mg

SESAME CANNA-CHICKEN SALAD WITH STRAWBERRY CANNA-SESAME DRESSING

This colorful grilled chicken salad is a fan favorite. It's the perfect balance of sweet and savory. The salad not only is light, simple to make, and chock-full of flavor, but also kicks in pretty quickly since the cannabinoids are in the dressing and are therefore easily metabolized.

SERVINGS

12

side salads / 6 entrées

PREP TIME

40

minutes

COOK TIME

8–10

minutes

APPROXIMATE THC PER SERVING*

10%:
2.5–5 mg

15%:
3.8–7.6 mg

20%:
5–10 mg

FOR THE CHICKEN AND MARINADE

6 boneless, skinless chicken breasts

¼ cup hoisin sauce

¼ cup barbecue sauce

½ teaspoon kosher salt

2 tablespoons sesame oil (plain)

½ cup water

FOR THE DRESSING

½ cup strawberries, muddled

2 tablespoons canna-sesame oil, plus 2 tablespoons toasted sesame oil

¼ cup sesame oil (plain)

3 tablespoons rice vinegar

¼ teaspoon dry mustard

1 teaspoon minced garlic

½ tablespoon strawberry jam

Pinch of salt and freshly ground black pepper

MARINATE THE CHICKEN

1   Pound the chicken breasts until the sides are even.

2   Mix the hoisin sauce, barbecue sauce, kosher salt, and plain sesame oil into ½ cup of water and stir well. Pour the mixture into a 1-gallon ziplock bag, then add the chicken and marinate in the refrigerator for at least 4 hours or overnight.

3   Grill for 4 to 5 minutes on each side. I like to rotate each side 45° halfway through cooking time. Remove from the grill and let cool 5 minutes. Cut chicken breasts into bite-size pieces.

MAKE THE DRESSING

4   Make the dressing by mixing all the ingredients together in a small bowl. Set aside to let the flavors develop.

recipe continues

FOR THE SALAD

3 cups kale, torn or as
    chiffonade (see sidebar,
    page 218)

3 cups baby greens

1 cup green cabbage,
    shredded

1 cup red cabbage,
    shredded

1 cup brussels sprouts,
    shredded

1 cup broccoli florets

2 blood oranges, divided
    into supremes (remove
    the membrane; see
    sidebar, below), or 1
    small can mandarin
    oranges

¾ cup strawberries, sliced

1 mango, diced

1 cup snow peas

1 Italian cucumber, sliced
    thin

½ package dry instant
    ramen noodles,
    crumbled

3 teaspoons sesame seeds

TO FINISH THE SALAD

5   Toss the kale, baby greens, green cabbage, red cabbage, brussels sprouts, and broccoli. Top with the marinated chicken, orange supremes, strawberries, mango, snow peas, and cucumber.

6   Drizzle with the salad dressing and sprinkle with crushed ramen noodles and sesame seeds before serving.

Approximate dose per serving is based on infusing 5 grams of cured/dried/decarbed cannabis into 5 ounces of oil.

KNIFE SKILLS:
ORANGE SUPREMES

Cut off top and bottom of orange so that its flesh is visible. Following the contour of the orange, cut the peel off the orange as close to the flesh as you can. Slice into each section as close to the membrane as possible. Each "supreme" should easily fall out.

KRAZY KALE & HEMP SEED SALAD WITH CURRIED ORANGE DRESSING

Between the citrus and avocado, this salad is California in a bowl. It's great for serving a crowd, and it's refreshing enough to eat nearly every day.

SERVINGS
12
side salads / 6 entrées

PREP TIME
30
minutes

APPROXIMATE THC PER SERVING*

10%:
2.5–5 mg

15%:
3.8–7.6 mg

20%:
5–10 mg

FOR THE SALAD

2 bunches kale

1 cup cherry tomatoes, halved (about ½ pint)

½ cup red onions, thinly sliced into half-moons

½ cup jicama, peeled and cubed (about ¼ pound)

1 cup seedless mandarin or navel orange, divided into supremes (remove the membrane; see sidebar, page 129), or 1 large can mandarin oranges, drained

2 avocados, sliced

1 tablespoon canna-oil, plus 1 tablespoon sesame oil

½ teaspoon sea salt

¼ cup hemp seed

Pomegranate seeds (optional, for some added color, sweetness, and crunch)

FOR THE DRESSING

1 cup orange juice (no pulp)

1 small garlic clove, minced

2 tablespoons apple cider vinegar

2 tablespoons canna-oil, plus 1 tablespoon sesame oil

¼ teaspoon dry mustard

½ teaspoon curry powder

1 Slice kale leaves off the stems and chop. Add the tomatoes, onions, jicama, and mandarin supremes, and toss.

2 Slice avocados into a separate bowl (put the pits in bowl to keep the avocados from turning brown). Drizzle the avocados with 2 tablespoons canna-sesame oil mixture. Add the avocados (remove the pits now) to the salad; sprinkle with salt and hemp seeds (and pomegranate seeds, if using).

3 Whisk together salad dressing ingredients. Drizzle the dressing over the salad and toss.

4 Sprinkle with additional hemp seeds, and serve.

Approximate dose per serving is based on infusing 5 grams of cured/dried/decarbed cannabis into 5 ounces of oil.

INFUSED PUMPKIN LAMB SOUP

SERVINGS
10

PREP TIME
45
minutes

COOK TIME
1
hour

APPROXIMATE
THC PER
SERVING*

| 10%: 4.6 mg |
| 15%: 6.8 mg |
| 20%: 9.2 mg |

This is one of my favorite fall recipes. Not only is it unique and quite tasty, but the presentation is a lot of fun. If you use a fresh pumpkin (instead of canned puree), you can create a fun serving bowl that is sure to get your guests oohing and aahing—and talking about your incredible soup for a long time to come.

1 medium pumpkin

Olive oil for sautéing

½ cup finely chopped sweet onion

2 pounds lamb neck with bones

Salt

2½ teaspoons minced garlic

⅓ cup sliced carrot, in rounds

⅓ cup sliced parsnip, in rounds

⅓ cup celery, sliced

2 tablespoons canna-butter

5 cups chicken stock

⅓ cup dark brown sugar

1 teaspoon ground cinnamon

¾ teaspoon ground ginger

½ teaspoon mace

1   Cut the top off the pumpkin (see sidebar, page 133), scoop out the seeds and set them aside, and throw out the fibers. Using a stiff metal spoon, scrape out ¼ inch of the flesh and cut into small pieces, if necessary.

2   Preheat large soup pot for 1 minute. Add enough olive oil to sauté. Add the onion and sauté until translucent.

3   Add the lamb and 1½ teaspoons salt. Continue to sauté until the lamb is lightly cooked and the onion is browned.

4   Add the garlic, carrot, parsnip, and celery. Stir and continue to sauté for about 2 minutes. Lower heat to simmer and add the canna-butter. Stir till melted and everything is coated.

5   Add chicken stock and bring to boil. Lower heat and add the pumpkin, brown sugar, cinnamon, ginger, mace, cloves, nutmeg, sea salt to taste, and 1 teaspoon pepper.

5 whole cloves

¼ teaspoon nutmeg

Sea salt

Freshly ground black
  pepper

¼ cup cornstarch

¾ cup half-and-half

6   Gently stir, then lower heat and simmer for 1 hour.

7   Preheat oven to 300°F.

8   Toss pumpkin seeds with a little olive oil and salt. Toast pumpkin seeds in oven for 20 minutes until crisp and barely brown along edges of seeds. Remove and set aside for garnish.

9   In a small bowl or measuring cup, stir cornstarch into half-and-half and add to simmering soup. Raise heat to medium; stir frequently. When soup thickens, reduce heat and simmer for 20 minutes. Salt and pepper to taste.

10   Transfer to "pumpkin serving bowl," garnish with roasted pumpkin seeds, replace "lid," and voilà!

Approximate dose per serving is based on infusing 5 grams of cured/dried/decarbed cannabis into 1⅓ sticks of butter.

HOW TO MAKE A

"PUMPKIN SERVING BOWL"

Use a sharp knife to slice a thin line all around the pumpkin approximately 2 inches below the stem. Using that as your guide, insert the knife into the pumpkin along the top of the line at a 45° angle. Repeat around pumpkin, every 1 inch, to create triangles. When you are done, it should look like jagged teeth all around the pumpkin. Lift top off pumpkin and your bowl is ready to go.

Infused Pumpkin
Lamb Soup, page
132

POTZO BALL SOUP

Try this contemporary twist on an old favorite. This is not your mama's matzo ball soup–but with the added THC and CBD, I'm sure she'll kvell with sheer delight. Tasty medicated matzo balls? What's not to love, bubby!

FOR THE BROTH

10 cups water

1 whole chicken, cut into eighths

1 beef bone (optional, for a heartier soup)

1 cup carrots, in rounds (reserve ½ cup)

1 cup celery, sliced (reserve ½ cup)

1 celery root, whole or halved to fit in pot

½ cup parsnip, cubed (reserve ¼ cup)

½ cup turnip, in rounds (reserve ¼ cup)

1 medium Spanish onion, diced

4 sprigs fresh dill (reserve 1 sprig)

1 bay leaf

¼ teaspoon turmeric

2 teaspoons black peppercorns

3 to 5 whole cloves

1 teaspoon kosher salt

1 Fill a large soup pot with 10 cups water.

2 Place the chicken, beef bone (if using), carrots, celery, celery root, parsnip, turnip, onion, and dill in a soup sock or wrap and tie in cheesecloth. Add bay leaf, turmeric, peppercorns, cloves, and salt. Bring to a boil, then reduce heat and simmer for 1 hour.

3 Remove the chicken and set aside.

4 Remove the vegetables and discard.

MAKE THE POTZO BALLS

5 In a medium bowl, mix together the matzo meal, baking powder, salt, and pepper.

6 In another bowl, whisk together eggs, canna-olive oil mixture, and seltzer or soda water.

7 Add dry ingredients to the wet ingredients and mix well.

8 Cover and refrigerate for 30 minutes.

recipe continues

1 cup matzo meal

2 teaspoons baking
   powder

Salt and pepper

4 eggs

1 tablespoon canna–olive
   oil, plus 3 tablespoons
   light olive oil

4 tablespoons seltzer or
   soda water

9 Bring the soup to a boil. Using an ice cream scoop for uniformity, drop matzo balls into the simmering soup. Add the reserved vegetables, reduce heat, and simmer for 30 minutes.

10 Shred the chicken and place it in serving bowls. Add the broth and potzo balls and serve immediately.

Approximate dose per serving is based on infusing 5 grams of cured/dried/decarbed cannabis into 5 ounces of oil.

FORBIDDEN FANTASY RICE

This is some pretty heady stuff: delicious, beautiful, and fast-acting. Because the canna-oil coats the rice and the rice doesn't absorb it, it will enter your system a lot faster than if it was cooked in. Go easy if you're using a high-THC strain.

SERVINGS
8

PREP TIME
10
minutes

COOK TIME
40
minutes

APPROXIMATE THC PER SERVING*

10%: 3.8 mg

15%: 5.7 mg

20%: 7.6 mg

3½ cups water

2 cups black forbidden rice

1 teaspoon fresh ginger, peeled and grated

1 clove garlic, minced

2 teaspoons kosher salt

1 tablespoon canna-coconut oil

2 teaspoons toasted sesame oil

¼ cup rice vinegar

1 pear, diced

¼ cup dried cherries

1   In a medium saucepan, bring the water, rice, ginger, garlic, and kosher salt to a boil over medium heat. Reduce the heat to a simmer, add the canna-coconut oil, and cover.

2   Cook until the rice is tender, about 30 minutes. Remove from the heat and let sit for 5 minutes, covered. Fluff with a fork and add the sesame oil, rice vinegar, pear, and cherries.

3   Transfer to serving bowl and serve warm.

Approximate dose per serving is based on infusing 5 grams of cured/dried/decarbed cannabis into 5 ounces of oil.

CANNA-GARLIC WASABI MASH (CAULIFLOWER, TURNIPS & PARSNIPS)

I love this take on mashed potatoes, which uses other root veggies along with wasabi and ginger for an exotic twist.

1 large head of garlic, whole

1 head cauliflower, florets

4 parsnips, cut into 1-inch pieces

4 turnips, cut into quarters

¼ teaspoon grated ginger

1 teaspoon wasabi powder

½ stick creamy canna-butter, softened, plus ½ stick grass-fed butter

½ cup milk

½ cup sour cream

Salt and freshly ground black pepper

1   Preheat oven to 400°F.

2   Wrap the garlic head in tinfoil and bake for 30 minutes.

3   Boil the cauliflower, parsnips, and turnips until soft, about 20 minutes. Transfer cooked vegetables to a large bowl (or drain water and leave vegetables in pot).

4   Squeeze the cloves of softened roasted garlic into the vegetables. Add the ginger, wasabi powder, and canna-butter mixture, then mash. Slowly add in the milk and sour cream. Continue mashing to desired consistency.

5   Add salt and pepper to taste, and serve.

Approximate dose per serving is based on infusing 5 grams of cured/dried/decarbed cannabis into 1⅓ sticks of butter.

SERVINGS
8

PREP TIME
45
minutes

COOK TIME
30
minutes

APPROXIMATE THC PER SERVING*

10%: 5.7 mg

15%: 8.6 mg

20%: 11.5 mg

CHARRED-TIP GLAZED BRUSSELS SPROUTS WITH CANNA-SESAME OIL

These are brussels sprouts with an Asian influence. The fish sauce and sesame oil add a rich, deep flavor that makes this dish stand out from the usual vegetable lineup.

2 cloves garlic, minced

¼ cup crushed raw peanuts

20 brussels sprouts, sliced in half lengthwise

3 teaspoons Vietnamese fish sauce

¼ cup non-infused sesame oil

2 tablespoons hoisin sauce

Crushed red pepper flakes

1 tablespoon canna-oil, plus 1 tablespoon toasted sesame oil

1   Preheat oven to 375°F. Gently toast half of the minced garlic and the crushed peanuts in a small pan over low heat until lightly browned and fragrant, 7 to 10 minutes. Remove and let cool.

2   While the peanuts and garlic are toasting, drizzle brussels sprouts with fish sauce, toss, and let marinate for 20 to 25 minutes.

3   In a small bowl, mix together the *non-infused* sesame oil, hoisin sauce, crushed red pepper flakes, and remaining garlic.

4   Drain the fish sauce from the brussels sprouts. Toss the *non-infused* sesame oil mixture in with the brussels sprouts, and transfer to a lightly greased large baking dish, cut side up. Bake for 12 to 15 minutes, until deeply browned but not quite charred.

5   Evenly drizzle the canna-oil mixture over the brussels sprouts and then flip.

6   Set oven to broil. Return the brussels sprouts to oven and bake for another 2 to 3 minutes until the outside of each begins to char. Watch carefully so they don't burn, and do not leave them in the oven for more than 3 more minutes.

7   Remove from the oven and add the toasted garlic and nuts. Toss until evenly coated, and serve.

SERVINGS
8

PREP TIME
30
minutes

COOK TIME
40–45
minutes total

APPROXIMATE THC PER SERVING*

10%: 3.8 mg

15%: 5.7 mg

20%: 7.6 mg

*Approximate dose per serving is based on infusing 5 grams of cured/dried/decarbed cannabis into 5 ounces of oil.

SWEET MANGO RICE

If you like Thai sticky rice, you'll love this deconstructed version of the original, which is not too sticky and not too sweet. With a little magical ingredient, it comes pretty close to perfection!

2 cups white rice

1 tablespoon canna-coconut oil

3 tablespoons extra-virgin coconut oil

4 cups salted water

1 cup unsweetened coconut milk

½ cup raw cane sugar

½ teaspoon salt

¼ cup sweetened shredded coconut

1 large mango, peeled, pitted, and cut into either slices or small cubes (whatever you prefer)

Juice of 1 lime

1 tablespoon sesame seeds, lightly toasted

1   In a medium saucepan, combine the rice, canna-coconut oil, and extra-virgin coconut oil with 4 cups of salted water. Bring to a boil, then immediately cover and reduce to a simmer. Cook until all the water is absorbed, about 20 minutes.

2   In a separate saucepan, bring the coconut milk, sugar, and salt to a boil. Remove from the heat and mix in shredded coconut.

3   When the rice is finished cooking, pour the coconut milk mixture over it and stir to combine. Cover the pot with a kitchen towel and replace the lid. Let the rice sit for about 40 minutes to absorb the coconut milk.

4   In the meantime, prepare the mango by combining it with the juice of 1 lime. Toss to cover thoroughly and let it sit for a few minutes to allow the flavors to develop.

5   When you're ready to serve, put the rice in a serving dish and top with the mango pieces. Sprinkle with sesame seeds, and voilà!

Approximate dose per serving is based on infusing 5 grams of cured/dried/decarbed cannabis into 5 ounces of oil.

SERVINGS
8

PREP TIME
15
minutes

COOK TIME
20
minutes

IDLE TIME
40
minutes

APPROXIMATE THC PER SERVING

10%: 3.8 mg

15%: 5.7 mg

20%: 7.6 mg

SPIKED SPANISH RICE SOUP

Warm, hearty, and mildly spicy, this zesty soup takes you on a comforting journey of acoustic guitars and Latin romance. Best served with tortilla chips or crostini.

SERVINGS
8

PREP TIME
20
minutes

COOK TIME
3
hours and 30
minutes

APPROXIMATE
THC PER
SERVING*

10%: 3.8 mg

15%: 5.7 mg

20%: 7.6 mg

10 plum tomatoes

2 tablespoons non-infused extra-virgin olive oil

2 teaspoons salt, plus more to taste

½ teaspoon freshly ground black pepper

¼ cup orzo

½ cup long-grain white rice

1 tablespoon canna-olive oil, plus 3 tablespoons extra-virgin olive oil

5 cups chicken stock

2 tablespoons fresh cilantro, finely chopped

1 large Spanish yellow onion, chopped

2 carrots, peeled and chopped

¼ cup celery, chopped

1 jalapeño pepper, thinly sliced

1½ teaspoons smoked sweet paprika

1 cup cooked shredded chicken

1   Preheat oven to 325°F.

2   Blanch and peel plum tomatoes by making a small X with a paring knife on the bottom end of each tomato. Bring a pot of water to a boil and submerge the tomatoes in the boiling water for 20 to 25 seconds until the X starts to peel away. Plunge the tomatoes into an ice bath for a minute. Start at the X and peel the skins off the tomatoes and discard. The peel should slide right off.

3   Toss the peeled whole tomatoes with 1 tablespoon of non-infused olive oil, 1 teaspoon salt, and the black pepper. Place in roasting pan. Roast tomatoes for 2 hours.

4   Add orzo and rice to canna-olive oil mixture and lightly toast for about 2 minutes, coating evenly. Add 1 cup of chicken stock and simmer for 20 minutes. Fluff rice and orzo, add the cilantro, and set aside.

5   In a large soup pot, sauté onion, carrots, celery, and jalapeño pepper with 1 teaspoon salt and paprika in the remaining 1 tablespoon of non-infused olive oil until onion is lightly browned.

½ cup sweet corn
4 cloves garlic, chopped
2 fresh bay leaves
Smoked salt

6   Add remaining 4 cups of chicken stock, shredded chicken, corn, garlic, and bay leaves. Bring to a boil, then reduce heat and simmer for 90 minutes. Remove the tomatoes from the oven and puree. Add tomato puree to the soup and continue to simmer for 30 minutes.

7   Place 2 tablespoons of the rice and orzo in each soup bowl, cover with soup, sprinkle with smoked salt, and voilà!

Approximate dose per serving is based on infusing 5 grams of cured/dried/decarbed cannabis into 5 ounces of oil.

CHAPTER NO. 6

Vegetarian Mains

CHICKPEA & EGGPLANT CANNA-TAJINE

This really fun and delicious collaboration with Chef Adrian Hale is a one-of-a-kind dish that will have your friends and family (even the non-vegetarian ones!) asking for more and begging for the recipe. You can make this and serve it in a Dutch oven—but for a beautiful and authentic presentation, it's worth investing in a tajine.

SERVINGS

8

PREP TIME

1

hour

COOK TIME

1

hour and 10 minutes

APPROXIMATE THC PER SERVING*

10%: 3.8 mg

15%: 5.7 mg

20%: 7.6 mg

7 cloves garlic, minced

4 teaspoons salt, plus more to taste

1-inch knob fresh ginger, grated

Small handful of fresh cilantro, destemmed and chopped (about 1 cup), plus more for garnish

Small handful of fresh parsley, destemmed and chopped (about 1 cup)

1 tablespoon canna–olive oil, plus 3 tablespoons extra-virgin olive oil

1 large eggplant

Olive oil for brushing eggplant

2 cups canned chickpeas, drained

1   Mince and mash the garlic with salt to create a paste. Add in the ginger, cilantro, and parsley and continue to mince and mash to create a paste. Transfer the paste into small bowl and mix with 4 tablespoons of the canna-olive oil mixture to create marinade.

2   Preheat oven to 400°F.

3   Slice the eggplant into 1-inch steaks. Cut a "crosshatch" diamond pattern into each side. Brush both sides of each steak with olive oil and sprinkle with salt. Place on lightly oiled cookie sheet and broil *each side* for 7 to 10 minutes. Eggplant steaks should appear dark brown and caramelized, but the flesh should still be firm. Remove and let cool.

4   Carefully slice off peel and cube the roasted eggplant. Place the eggplant cubes and chickpeas in a large bowl and add garlic paste marinade. Toss and refrigerate for at least 2 hours.

1 (8-ounce) jar oil-packed sun-dried tomatoes

28-ounce-can whole peeled tomatoes, drained

Generous pinch of saffron

2 tablespoons hot water

2 teaspoon cinnamon

2 teaspoons turmeric

½ teaspoon freshly ground black pepper

Good grating of fresh nutmeg

¼ cup honey

2 red onions, sliced

1 lemon

¼ cup yogurt, for garnish

¼ cup almonds, toasted and roughly chopped

5 or 6 Medjool dates, pitted and cut into small pieces

5   Combine the whole jar of sun-dried tomatoes (including the oil), drained whole tomatoes, and 1 teaspoon of salt in a food processor and puree until smooth. Place the mixture in a medium saucepan over medium heat and simmer until sticky and reduced by half, about 30 minutes. Stir occasionally so the paste doesn't stick to the bottom of the pot and burn.

6   While the tomatoes are cooking, put a pinch of saffron in 2 tablespoons of hot water and let it steep for at least 20 minutes.

7   Remove the tomato jam from the heat and add saffron water, cinnamon, turmeric, black pepper, nutmeg, and honey.

8   Preheat oven to 340°F.

9   Scatter sliced red onions on the bottom of an 11- to 12-inch tajine or similar-sized Dutch oven. Pour the tomato jam over the onions. Cut the lemon in half and squeeze the juice onto the tomato-and-onion mixture. Toss to coat.

10   Place the marinated eggplant and chickpeas on top, and cover with the lid.

11   Bake for 1 hour and 15 minutes, until the onions are soft and saucelike. Uncover and raise the heat to broil for about 5 minutes until eggplant and chickpeas are lightly browned on top.

12   To serve, add a dollop of yogurt, and then jauntily scatter the almonds, dates, and reserved cilantro over the top.

Approximate dose per serving is based on infusing 5 grams of cured/dried/decarbed cannabis into 5 ounces of oil.

INFUSED WILD MUSHROOM RISOTTO

This collaboration with Google Chef J. P. Reyes is rich and buttery and serves as a great main dish for vegetarians. You can substitute the canna-butter with canna–coconut oil (not extra-virgin coconut oil, though, because of its pronounced coconut flavor) to make this dish vegan.

☆

SERVINGS
8

PREP TIME
30
minutes

APPROXIMATE
THC PER
SERVING*

10%: 6.6 mg

15%: 10 mg

20%: 13.2 mg

FOR THE MUSHROOMS

3 tablespoons extra-virgin olive oil

¾ cup wild mushrooms

Salt and freshly ground black pepper

¾ cup cremini mushrooms, left whole if small, otherwise quartered

1 medium garlic clove, peeled

1 tablespoon grass-fed butter

1 medium shallot, minced

2 teaspoons fresh thyme, chopped

2 teaspoons Italian parsley, chopped

1 tablespoon tomato paste

½ cup white wine

3 cups vegetable stock

2 cups water

1 tablespoon canna-butter

TO COOK THE MUSHROOMS

1   Heat a wide sauté pan over high heat and add 1 tablespoon of extra-virgin olive oil to coat the pan. Add the wild mushrooms to cover the bottom of the pan in a flat layer. Season with salt and pepper and sauté until lightly brown and cooked through.

2   Transfer the mushrooms to a colander and repeat the above step with an additional 1 tablespoon of olive oil and the cremini mushrooms.

3   Smash the garlic clove and smear it with a pinch of salt to make a paste. Add the garlic to the pan with 1 tablespoon of butter, the remaining 1 tablespoon olive oil, shallot, thyme, and parsley. Cover and cook gently over low heat until the shallot and garlic are soft.

4   Uncover and stir in the tomato paste and cook slowly for about 5 minutes. Stir the mushrooms back into the pan, and add the white wine. Raise the heat to medium-high, and cook until the wine is mostly evaporated.

recipe continues

1 tablespoon canna–olive oil, plus 1 tablespoon extra-virgin olive oil

Juice of 1 lemon

FOR THE RISOTTO

5 cups vegetable stock

1 large yellow onion, diced

4 tablespoons grass-fed butter

1 tablespoon extra-virgin olive oil

2 cups Arborio rice

¾ cup white wine

Salt

Parmesan cheese (optional)

Add the vegetable stock and water and bring to a boil. Immediately lower to a simmer. Cook until the liquid is reduced by half. It should be thick enough to coat the back of a spoon.

5   Remove from the heat and add in canna-butter and canna–olive oil mixture.

6   Adjust seasoning with salt, pepper, and lemon, if needed.

TO COOK THE RISOTTO

7   Bring the stock to a boil, and then lower to a simmer.

8   In a saucepot, combine the onion, 1 tablespoon butter, and olive oil and cook covered over low heat. Cook until the onion is soft and translucent, but with no color.

9   Add the rice and turn the heat to medium. Toast for a couple of minutes and add the wine. Raise heat to high until the wine boils and then lower to a simmer. Cook until the wine reduces by half and then add a generous ladleful of stock. Adjust heat to a simmer. Season with a pinch of salt a little at a time as needed.

10   Keep stirring and adding stock, a little at a time, until the rice is al dente (cooked yet firm), 20 to 30 minutes. Stir in 3 tablespoons of grass-fed butter and cover. Allow to rest for a few minutes.

11   To serve, transfer the risotto to a bowl and cover with wild mushrooms and (if using) Parmesan.

*Approximate dose per serving is based on infusing 5 grams of cured/dried/decarbed cannabis into 1⅓ sticks of butter.

INFUSED FIRE-ROASTED VEGGIES

These veggies are simple and delicious. To keep the cannabis flavor at the right level, the trick is to drizzle the canna–olive oil only on the zucchini and bell peppers. The distinct flavor of both vegetables works incredibly well with the mild cannabis flavor in your oil.

SERVINGS
8

PREP TIME
30
minutes

COOK TIME
15
minutes

APPROXIMATE THC PER SERVING*

10%: 3.8 mg

15%: 5.7 mg

20%: 7.6 mg

4 medium potatoes, sliced into 1-inch-thick rounds

1 red bell pepper, sliced into 1-inch strips

1 green bell pepper, sliced into 1-inch strips

1 yellow bell pepper, sliced into 1-inch strips

1 orange bell pepper, sliced into 1-inch strips

2 large white onions, sliced into ½-inch rounds

3 green zucchini, cut lengthwise in ¼-inch slices

3 yellow zucchini, cut lengthwise in ¼-inch slices

1 pound asparagus, cut into ½-inch pieces

2 cloves garlic, minced

¼ cup extra-virgin olive oil

2 or 3 tablespoons sea salt

1 teaspoon crushed black pepper

½ teaspoon dried oregano

3 sprigs fresh thyme, destemmed

1 tablespoons canna–olive oil, plus 3 tablespoons light olive oil

1   Preheat grill on medium to 400°F.

2   Put all the vegetables in a large ziplock bag. Add the garlic, extra-virgin olive oil, salt, pepper, oregano, and thyme. Shake to coat evenly. Remove vegetables from ziplock bag and place them directly on the grill or vegetable-grilling tray. Cover grill and roast for 12 to 15 minutes, until there are dark caramelized grill lines on the vegetables.

3   Carefully drizzle the canna–olive oil mixture on the zucchini and bell peppers only. Continue to roast for 1 more minute.

4   Remove to a serving platter.

Approximate dose per serving is based on infusing 5 grams of cured/dried/decarbed cannabis into 5 ounces of oil.

CANNA-CHILI TARRAGON CAULIFLOWER

This new collaboration with Chef J. P. Reyes is another favorite of mine! The chilies rise to the occasion to complement the light herbal flavors of the cannabis, tarragon, and parsley. It hits pretty quickly because the canna-olive oil is drizzled to coat the cauliflower at the end rather than cooked in as you fry the cauliflower.

2 heads cauliflower, cut into florets

¼ cup cornstarch

2 cups light olive oil

Salt

2 teaspoons chili flakes

⅓ cup capers

1 tablespoon extra-virgin olive oil

3 cloves garlic, thinly sliced

2 sprigs Italian parsley, destemmed and roughly chopped

6 sprigs tarragon, destemmed and roughly chopped

1 tablespoon canna-olive oil, plus ¼ cup extra-virgin olive oil

3 Calabrian chilies, sliced

½ cup coarse breadcrumbs

1   Wash cauliflower and cradle in a dishtowel to remove excess water. Toss cauliflower florets in cornstarch to coat. Shake off excess and set aside.

2   Preheat a wide shallow frying pan over high heat. Fill with about 1 inch of light olive oil and lower the heat to medium.

3   Add the cauliflower florets cut side down. Season with salt and panfry over medium-high heat. As it cooks, turn each piece so all sides brown evenly. It's okay if the florets are crowded; it will create steam and help them cook through. Fry until evenly browned. Place in a colander to drain. Sprinkle with chili flakes.

4   Add the capers to the remaining hot oil in the frying pan and fry for about 1 minute until they puff up a little. Using a slotted spoon, remove the toasted capers to a plate lined with paper towels.

5   Discard the light olive oil and add extra-virgin olive oil to the pan. Add the garlic, parsley, tarragon, and toasted capers and cook over medium heat. Stir until the garlic is browned. Remove from the heat and add canna-olive oil mixture. Add cauliflower back to the pan and toss. Adjust seasoning if needed.

6   Transfer to a bowl, garnish with Calabrian chili and breadcrumbs, and serve.

SERVINGS
8

PREP TIME
15
minutes

COOK TIME
5–7
minutes

APPROXIMATE THC PER SERVING*
10%: 3.8 mg
15%: 5.7 mg
20%: 7.6 mg

*Approximate dose per serving is based on infusing 5 grams of cured/dried/decarbed cannabis into 5 ounces of oil.

420 CHEF QUINOA WITH CANDIED EGGPLANT BACON (VEGAN)

This eggplant bacon will win over all of your vegetarian friends. The quinoa is simple but includes a nice variety of ingredients to brighten things up. Note: For cherry "bacon" use cherry syrup instead of maple syrup or combined with maple syrup.

SERVINGS
8

PREP TIME
25
minutes

COOK TIME
30
minutes

APPROXIMATE THC PER SERVING*

10%: 7.6 mg

15%: 11.4 mg

20%: 15.2 mg

2 tablespoons extra-virgin olive oil

1 red onion, chopped

1 cup acorn squash, cubed small

1 cup brussels sprouts, shredded

2 cloves garlic

1 cup quinoa, rinsed

1½ teaspoons salt

1 teaspoon freshly ground black pepper

1¼ cups low-sodium vegetable broth

2 tablespoons canna–olive oil, plus 2 tablespoons light olive oil

½ cup Candied Eggplant Bacon, crumbled (see sidebar, page 159)

1   In a Dutch oven over medium heat, add the olive oil and red onion. Cook and stir the onion until translucent, about 5 minutes. Add the squash, brussels sprouts, and garlic and sauté until the squash is lightly caramelized, about 10 minutes.

2   Add the quinoa, salt, and pepper. Reduce heat to medium-low; cook, stirring, until the quinoa becomes light brown in color and has a toasted fragrance, 5 to 7 minutes. Slowly pour in the vegetable broth. Bring the mixture back to a boil over medium heat. Add the canna–olive oil mixture, reduce heat to medium-low, and cover. Simmer for 30 minutes until all the liquid is absorbed.

3   Fluff with fork, top with eggplant bacon crumbles, and serve.

Candied Eggplant Bacon

PREP TIME

25

minutes, plus
1–2 hours to
marinate

COOK TIME

15

minutes

1 small eggplant

½ teaspoon liquid smoke (a liquid flavoring sold in most grocery stores)

1 tablespoon dark cherry syrup from Luxardo Original Maraschino or Amarena cherries, or maple syrup

2 tablespoons coconut oil

1 teaspoon paprika

1 teaspoon sea salt

½ teaspoon crushed black pepper

¼ cup all-purpose flour

1   Using a mandoline, slice the eggplant into "bacon" strips.

2   In a large bowl, combine the liquid smoke, your syrup of choice, 1 tablespoon coconut oil, paprika, salt, and pepper. Stir to mix. Add the eggplant strips, coat evenly, and marinate for 1 to 2 hours. Transfer to paper towels to remove excess moisture.

3   Preheat a skillet and add the remaining 1 tablespoon coconut oil to fry.

4   Dredge the "bacon" strips in the flour.

5   Fry the "bacon" until crispy and serve crumbled over the quinoa.

Approximate dose per serving is based on infusing 5 grams of cured/dried/decarbed cannabis into 5 ounces of oil.

CANNA-COWBOY SALAD

This is another party favorite that packs a punch and kicks in fairly quickly. The flavor here is southwestern meets fresh California cuisine. The cashews and cilantro contrast with the starchiness of the beans and corn, making each flavor stand out in every bite.

FOR THE DRESSING

2 tablespoons canna–olive oil, plus 2 tablespoons light olive oil

¼ cup red wine vinegar

¼ cup raw cane sugar

Juice of ½ lime

2 cloves garlic, minced or pressed

2 tablespoons adobo sauce from canned chipotle peppers

½ teaspoon cumin

Salt

FOR THE SALAD

3 (15-ounce) cans black beans, rinsed and drained

2 (15-ounce) cans black-eyed peas, rinsed and drained

1 (15-ounce) can chickpeas, rinsed and drained

4 (15-ounce) cans whole kernel corn

¼ cup finely chopped red onion

¼ cup finely chopped green onions, tops only

¼ cup sweet Vidalia onion (or similar), diced

¼ cup red pepper, diced

¼ cup yellow (and/or orange) pepper, diced

1 small jalapeño pepper, minced

1 chipotle pepper (canned in adobo sauce), chopped

½ cup chopped cilantro

SERVINGS

16

PREP TIME

20

minutes

COOK TIME

5

minutes

IDLE TIME

8+

hours

APPROXIMATE THC PER SERVING*

10%: 3.8 mg

15%: 5.6 mg

20%: 7.6 mg

½ cup raw roasted
cashews, lightly
crushed

¼ cup chopped cilantro

Red pepper flakes

1   In a saucepot combine the canna–olive oil mixture, vinegar, and sugar over medium heat. Bring to a boil, and stir for 1 minute while boiling, then immediately remove from the heat (this is important for maintaining the integrity of the canna–olive oil).

2   Add in the rest of the dressing ingredients, mix, and let cool thoroughly (at least 1 hour so you don't cook the vegetables in the salad).

3   In a large glass bowl, combine all the salad ingredients. Drizzle the dressing over the salad, toss, and marinate overnight.

4   Garnish with the roasted cashews, cilantro, and red pepper flakes before serving.

Approximate dose per serving is based on infusing 5 grams of cured/dried/decarbed cannabis into 5 ounces of oil.

TRICOLOR CANNA-BEET & WATERMELON SALAD

Don't let this crisp, refreshing, and colorful salad fool you. It'll pull you in with its beauty and keep you wanting more with its taste. But go easy, as it packs a powerful punch that'll hit you pretty quickly. I like to start my summer meals with this one, as it's a perfectly dosed appetizer salad that kicks things into gear.

FOR THE SALAD

4 medium red beets, tops removed and scrubbed

4 medium golden beets, tops removed and scrubbed

1 cup seedless watermelon, cubed small

4 ounces feta cheese, crumbled

2 tablespoons cilantro, chopped

Maldon sea salt and freshly ground coarse black pepper

FOR THE DRESSING

½ cup balsamic vinegar

1 tablespoon canna-olive oil, plus 3 tablespoons light olive oil

2 teaspoons spicy mustard

1 teaspoon fresh lime juice

1 teaspoon honey

1   Preheat oven to 400ºF.

2   Wrap the beets in foil and bake for 50 to 55 minutes, until tender but still firm. Remove the beets from the foil and refrigerate for 1 hour. Peel the cold beets and cut into small cubes.

3   To make the dressing, whisk together the vinegar, canna-olive oil mixture, mustard, lime juice, and honey. Set aside.

4   Toss the beets and the watermelon together. Sprinkle with crumbled feta cheese and cilantro. Evenly cover with dressing and toss.

5   Garnish with a pinch or two of Maldon sea salt and pepper before serving.

Approximate dose per serving is based on infusing 5 grams of cured/dried/decarbed cannabis into 5 ounces of oil.

SERVINGS
8

PREP TIME
30
minutes

COOK TIME
55
minutes

APPROXIMATE THC PER SERVING*

10%: 3.8 mg

15%: 5.7 mg

20%: 7.6 mg

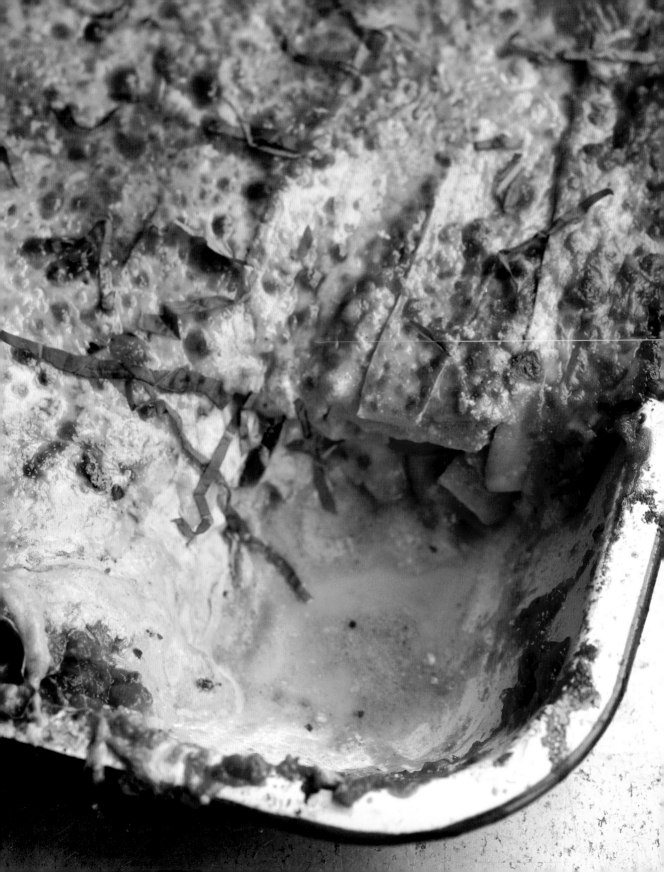

INFUSED FIRE-ROASTED VEGGIE LASAGNA

Lasagna infused with cannabis? Now we're talking! This is definitely not your (or my) mama's lasagna, but trust me, she'll love it . . . and she'll love you for it. Mine certainly does!

SERVINGS
8

PREP TIME
40
minutes

COOK TIME
1
hour and 10
minutes

APPROXIMATE
THC PER
SERVING*
10%: 7.6 mg
15%: 11.4 mg
20%: 15.2 mg

1 large white onion, diced

2 red bell peppers, halved, seeded, and deribbed

3 green zucchini, cut lengthwise in ¼-inch-thick slices

3 yellow summer squash, cut lengthwise in ¼-inch-thick slices

1 Japanese eggplant, cut lengthwise in ¼-inch-thick slices

3 cloves garlic, minced

¼ cup extra-virgin olive oil

2 teaspoons sea salt, plus more to taste

Crushed black pepper

1 teaspoon fresh oregano, destemmed

2 tablespoons canna–olive oil

8 ounces cream cheese, at room temperature

16 ounces fresh whole-milk ricotta cheese

2 extra-large eggs, lightly beaten

4 cups your favorite marinara sauce

1   Turn the oven on broil.

2   Put the onion, red peppers, zucchini, summer squash, and eggplant in a large ziplock bag. Add 2 cloves of minced garlic, extra-virgin olive oil, 1 teaspoon sea salt, black pepper, and oregano. Shake to coat.

3   Place the vegetables in a roasting pan, making sure that the zucchini and eggplant don't overlap and that the peppers are skin side up. Roast for 12 to 15 minutes, until the skin is somewhat charred but not burned. Keep a close eye on the eggplant and zucchini. Remove from oven and let cool.

4   Peel the peppers.

5   Drizzle the canna-oil on the roasted veggies and set aside.

6   Place the cream cheese, half a grilled pepper, remaining 1 clove minced garlic, and 1 teaspoon salt in a food processor. Pulse until well blended.

7   In a large bowl, combine pepper-and-cream cheese mixture, ricotta cheese, and eggs. Add salt and pepper to taste.

8   Preheat oven to 340°F.

recipe continues

1 package no-boil lasagna
  noodles

1 cup freshly grated
  Parmesan cheese

1 pound lightly salted
  fresh mozzarella,
  shredded

¼ cup fresh basil, chopped
  or as chiffonade (see
  sidebar, page 218)

9   Pour enough marinara sauce on the bottom of a large baking dish
to cover the bottom. Place a layer of uncooked lasagna noodles on top
of marinara sauce. Sprinkle some Parmesan on top of the sauce. Layer
ricotta mixture, veggies, mozzarella, and sauce. Place a layer of uncooked
noodles on top and repeat until three-quarters from top of dish. Top with
remaining sauce and mozzarella. Sprinkle with rest of Parmesan.

10   Bake 40 to 45 minutes until golden brown. Garnish with chopped basil
or chiffonade, and serve.

*Approximate dose per serving is based on infusing 5 grams of cured/dried/decarbed cannabis
into 5 ounces of oil.*

BUZZED CHICKPEA CURRY & CANNA-BUTTERED SAFFRON RICE

The flavors in this dish will send your taste buds on a journey, from the cumin to the saffron to the garlic to the curry—and depending on the strain you use, it could send your head on a journey as well.

2 (15-ounce) cans chickpeas, drained

3 cloves garlic, minced

½ teaspoon freshly ground black pepper

3 pods fresh cardamom, crushed

1 tablespoon canna-olive oil, plus 1 tablespoon light olive oil

4 tablespoons olive oil

½ white onion, chopped

3 potatoes, peeled and cubed

2 teaspoons salt

1 cup green peas

½ cup sun-dried tomatoes, diced

½ teaspoon turmeric

1 teaspoon fresh ginger, grated

7 cups vegetable stock

1   In a medium bowl, combine the chickpeas, garlic, freshly ground pepper, cardamom, and canna-olive oil mixture. Let marinate for at least 2 hours.

2   In a large pot, heat 1 tablespoon of olive oil and sauté the onion and potatoes and 1 teaspoon salt until onion is caramelized and outsides of potato cubes are light to medium brown.

3   Add the green peas, sun-dried tomatoes, turmeric, and ginger. Continue to gently sauté for 2 minutes.

4   Add 3½ cups vegetable stock, ½ teaspoon cumin, chili, bay leaf, cinnamon stick, and curry powder. Bring to boil. Reduce heat and simmer for 1 hour. Remove from the stovetop and mix in the yogurt and marinated chickpeas. Cover and let sit for 20 minutes.

5   Rinse the rice in mesh strainer until the water runs clear.

recipe continues

1 teaspoon cumin seeds

1 red chili

1 bay leaf

1 cinnamon stick

1 teaspoon yellow curry powder

3 tablespoons yogurt

2 cups white long-grain rice

1 teaspoon sugar

5 to 7 saffron threads

2 tablespoons creamy canna-butter, plus 2 tablespoons salted grass-fed butter

½ cup plain Greek yogurt (for garnish)

2 teaspoons cilantro or parsley, chopped (for garnish)

6   In a medium pot, add the remaining cumin seeds to the rest of the non-infused olive oil. Heat on medium until cumin seeds are toasted and fragrant, 1 to 1½ minutes.

7   Add rice and sugar. Stir until rice becomes lightly toasted and caramelized. Add the remaining vegetable stock, remaining salt, and saffron. Bring to a boil. Reduce heat to simmer, cover, and cook for 20 minutes on low.

8   Fluff and incorporate the creamy canna-butter mixture.

9   Top with the chickpea-potato mixture, and garnish with yogurt and cilantro or parsley.

Approximate dose per serving is based on infusing 5 grams of cured/dried/decarbed cannabis into 5 ounces of oil or 1⅓ sticks of butter.

FAKIN' "BAKIN'" VEGGIE CHEESEBURGER

No vegetarian section would be complete without a "cheeseburger," and I love the flavor of the chipotle combined with the tarragon in this version. Top things off with some Candied Eggplant Bacon (page 159) and Lime-Chipotle Canna-Aioli (page 54), and you've got a rockin' veggie burger on your hands.

FOR THE BURGER

¼ cup sweet onion, diced

¼ cup light olive oil

Salt and freshly ground black pepper

1 tablespoon canna–olive oil, plus 3 tablespoons light olive oil

¼ cup chives, minced

4 cloves garlic, minced

¼ cup tarragon, minced

2 tablespoons red bell pepper, diced small

1 (15-ounce) can black beans, drained and mashed

1 (15-ounce) can chickpeas, drained and mashed

2 chipotle peppers in adobo sauce, minced

1½ cups rolled oats

½ teaspoon paprika

½ teaspoon celery salt

3 eggs or vegan egg substitute

1   In a medium pan, sauté onion with light olive oil and a sprinkling of salt and pepper until caramelized.

2   In a large bowl, mix together the caramelized onion with the remainder of the burger ingredients. Using your hands, mash and knead until everything is thoroughly combined. Divide "burger meat" into 4 equal portions.

3   Oil your hands with a little olive oil and make patties that are about 1 inch thick. Place them on a plate lined with paper towel and cover them with plastic wrap. Refrigerate for 30 minutes.

4   Cover the bottom of a skillet with olive oil. Cook the patties 2 to 3 minutes per side until lightly browned.

5   Serve on whole-wheat buns topped with cheese, Candied Eggplant Bacon (page 159), lettuce, tomato, and Lime-Chipotle Canna-Aioli (page 54) for a complete experience.

Approximate dose per serving is based on infusing 5 grams of cured/dried/decarbed cannabis into 5 ounces of oil.

SERVINGS
4

PREP TIME
40
minutes

COOK TIME
5–6
minutes

IDLE TIME
30
minutes

APPROXIMATE THC PER SERVING (DOES NOT INCLUDE AIOLI)*

10%: 7.6 mg

15%: 11.4 mg

20%: 15.2 mg

TO FINISH

Whole-wheat buns

Pepper jack and/or chipotle cheddar cheese

Candied Eggplant Bacon (page 159)

Lettuce for garnish

1 tomato, sliced for garnish

Lime-Chipotle Canna-Aioli (page 54)

ZUCCHINI CANNA-KUGEL WITH CARAMELIZED LEEKS

This is Grandma's kugel—with a twist! While it stands well on its own, this dish is also great served alongside Canna-Beer Chicken (page 180, for the meat eaters).

Olive oil for sautéing and greasing pan

2 leeks, sliced

2 medium shallots, sliced thin

½ teaspoon fresh marjoram

Salt

Coarsely ground black pepper

2 medium zucchini, grated into shreds

2 large carrots, grated into shreds

3 large Yukon Gold potatoes, grated into shreds

3 large eggs, beaten

1 tablespoon canna-olive oil, plus 3 tablespoons light olive oil

3 tablespoons seasoned breadcrumbs

1   Preheat a large skillet and add olive oil to sauté.

2   Sauté the leeks and shallots with marjoram, salt, and pepper to taste, until lightly browned. Remove and cool.

3   Preheat oven to 325°F. Grease a 9-by-13-inch casserole dish and set aside.

4   In a large bowl, mix the shredded zucchini, carrots, potatoes, eggs, canna-olive oil mixture, and salt. Add caramelized leeks and shallots. Sprinkle in breadcrumbs and combine. Add salt and pepper to taste.

5   Pour mixture into the prepared casserole dish. Bake for 1 hour until set and the edges are lightly browned, and serve warm.

Approximate dose per serving is based on infusing 5 grams of cured/dried/decarbed cannabis into 5 ounces of oil.

SERVINGS
8

PREP TIME
15
minutes

COOK TIME
1
hour

APPROXIMATE THC PER SERVING*

10%: 3.8 mg

15%: 5.7 mg

20%: 7.6 mg

Infused BBQ Pulled Brisket, page 176

CHAPTER NO. 7

Meat & Fish Mains

INFUSED BBQ PULLED BRISKET

This is a Crock-"Pot" recipe at its finest. It's an easy recipe, and it's always nice coming home to a fragrant meal at the end of the day.

SERVINGS
10

PREP TIME
20
minutes

COOK TIME
10
hours

APPROXIMATE
THC PER
SERVING*

10%: 6 mg

15%: 9 mg

20%: 12 mg

1 teaspoon onion powder

½ teaspoon garlic powder

½ teaspoon cumin

½ teaspoon chili powder

1 tablespoon paprika

½ teaspoon cayenne pepper

1 tablespoon kosher salt

Coarsely ground black pepper

1 large onion, sliced into ½-inch-thick rings

1 brisket, 4 to 5 pounds, first cut

1½ cups ketchup

2 teaspoons honey

1 teaspoon liquid smoke

½ cup brown sugar

¾ cup water

3 tablespoons cider vinegar

2 tablespoons canna–olive oil, plus 2 tablespoons light olive oil

10 whole-wheat buns

1 large red onion, sliced

2 cups lettuce, shredded

3 beefsteak tomatoes, sliced

1   In a small bowl, mix together the onion powder, garlic powder, cumin, chili powder, paprika, cayenne pepper, kosher salt, and black pepper.

2   Place the onion on the bottom of a Crock-Pot or slow cooker.

3   Rub the brisket with dry spice mix. Place the meat on top of the onion in the Crock-Pot.

4   In a large measuring cup, mix the ketchup, honey, liquid smoke, brown sugar, water, and cider vinegar. Pour the sauce evenly over the brisket.

5   Cover and cook on low for 10 hours (or on high for 6 hours).

6   Transfer the brisket to a cutting board and use two forks to shred the meat.

7   Pour the canna–olive oil mixture over the pulled brisket, smother with gravy, and toss.

8   Serve on whole-wheat buns topped with red onion, lettuce, and tomato.

*Approximate dose per serving is based on infusing 5 grams of cured/dried/decarbed cannabis into 5 ounces of oil.

NOTE

If your Crock–Pot burns hot, you may have to add water toward the end of the cooking time so that your brisket doesn't burn.

BRAISED CANNA-BEEF STROGANOFF WITH WILD MUSHROOMS

This is the ultimate comfort food and the perfect recipe to warm you on a cold winter night. Snuggle up with a bowl and enjoy!

SERVINGS

6

PREP TIME

45

minutes

COOK TIME

2

hours and 30 minutes

APPROXIMATE THC PER SERVING*

10%: 5.7 mg

15%: 8.5 mg

20%: 11.4 mg

3 pounds chuck steak or short ribs, cubed

Salt and freshly ground black pepper

3 tablespoons flour

Olive oil

1 medium onion, diced small

2 carrots, diced small

2 stalks celery, diced small

¼ cup dry red wine (you can use any dry red; I prefer burgundy or zinfandel)

1 cup beef broth

1 sprig rosemary

5 sprigs thyme

1 bay leaf

1½ tablespoons canna-butter, plus 2½ tablespoons grass-fed butter

1½ cup mixed mushrooms, quartered (I mix portabello, shiitake, and cremini)

1   Preheat oven to 325°F.

2   Season the beef cubes with salt and pepper, then coat them with flour.

3   Preheat a Dutch oven or large pot with a tight-fitting lid on high heat. Add enough olive oil to coat the bottom of the pot.

4   Brown beef cubes so all sides are lightly browned. Don't crowd the pot; you can do this in batches, if needed. Remove browned beef with a slotted spoon and set aside.

5   Lower the heat to medium and add the onion, carrots, and celery. Sauté until browned. When vegetables are browned, add some of the wine and use a wooden spoon to deglaze the bottom of the pot by stirring and loosening the bits at the bottom.

6   Return the meat to the pot, and add enough beef broth just to cover—about 1 cup. Add the rosemary, thyme, and bay leaf. Cover the pot and cook in the oven for 2 hours.

7   While waiting for the stew to cook, in a separate pan, sauté mushrooms and shallots with some of the canna-butter mixture for 3– 5 minutes, until the shallots are soft and translucent. Add a splash or two of wine to deglaze.

2 shallots, sliced thin

1 cup sour cream

1 package broad egg
noodles

Flat-leaf parsley, to garnish
(optional)

8   When the meat is finished cooking—it should be soft and fork tender—remove the herb sprigs and bay leaf. Add the shallot-and-mushroom mixture, then the sour cream. Mix to incorporate. Adjust the seasonings, adding salt and pepper to taste.

9   Cook the noodles in a large pot of boiling salted water until tender, about 8 minutes. Drain. Transfer to a bowl. Add the remaining cannabutter and toss to coat. Season with salt and pepper to taste.

10   Divide the noodles evenly onto 6 plates. Top with beef and sauce, garnish with parsley, if using, and serve.

*Approximate dose per serving is based on infusing 5 grams of cured/dried/decarbed cannabis into 1⅓ sticks of butter.

CANNA-BEER CHICKEN

My variation on the popular beer-can chicken takes this dish to a new level. Propped on a beer can, the chicken roasts beautifully and browns evenly. Couple that with the canna-olive oil and spices, and this chicken is elevated from a basic recipe to a fun dinner party entrée any night of the week.

1 can dark beer

½ cup olive oil

¼ cup lemon juice

4 cloves garlic, minced

1 chipotle pepper in adobo sauce, diced

3 teaspoons kosher salt

1 whole chicken (4 to 5 pounds)

2 teaspoons dry mustard

1 teaspoon dried basil

2 teaspoons dried thyme

½ teaspoon dried fennel

½ teaspoon cayenne pepper

1 tablespoon paprika

1 teaspoon coarsely ground black pepper

1 large onion, sliced

½ cup water

1 tablespoon canna-olive oil, plus 3 tablespoons light olive oil

1   Pour half the can of beer into a large ziplock bag; save the rest of the beer in the can and set aside.

2   Add the ½ cup olive oil, lemon juice, garlic, and chipotle pepper to the bag. Slowly add 2 teaspoons of kosher salt. The marinade will foam, so be careful not to mix it together too quickly.

3   Place the chicken in the bag and push the air out while sealing the bag tightly. Let marinate for at least 4 hours, redistributing the liquid around the chicken every now and then.

4   When you're ready to cook, preheat oven to 350°F.

5   In a small bowl, combine the dry mustard, basil, thyme, fennel seeds, cayenne pepper, paprika, black pepper, and the remaining 1 tablespoon kosher salt. Set aside.

6   Remove the chicken from the marinade; retain the liquid. Place your hand under the skin of the chicken to separate the skin from the flesh, but don't remove it. Rub the chicken with the spice mix *under* the skin. Save some spice mix for outside of chicken. Use the marinade to rub the entire outside of the chicken, then sprinkle the remaining spice mix on the outside of the chicken.

SERVINGS
6

PREP TIME
30
minutes

COOK TIME
1½–2
hours

IDLE TIME
4
hours

APPROXIMATE THC PER SERVING*

10%: 5 mg

15%: 7.6mg

20%: 10 mg

7   Now for the fun part: In a roasting pan, stand the chicken upright on top of the half-filled beer can.

8   Add onion around pan and ½ cup of water. Roast for 22 minutes per pound.

9   Now for the tricky part: Remove the chicken from the can and set it breast side down in a clean pan. Use a baster to add the canna–olive oil mixture under the skin all around the chicken. Cover with gravy and onion.

10 Lower the oven to 325°F and bake for 10 more minutes.

11 Remove the chicken from the oven and let it sit for 15 to 20 minutes before carving and serving.

Approximate dose per serving is based on infusing 5 grams of cured/dried/decarbed cannabis into 5 ounces of oil.

Canna-Beer Chicken, page 180

CANNA-CHICKEN TARRAGON WITH MUSHROOMS

As you can probably tell, I love tarragon—and mushrooms! Pair this with a slice of Zucchini Canna-Kugel (page 173) and you're on your way to canna-bliss.

SERVINGS
4

PREP TIME
30
minutes

COOK TIME
30
minutes

APPROXIMATE
THC PER
SERVING*

10%: 5.7 mg
15%: 8.6 mg
20%: 11.5 mg

3 cloves garlic, chopped

¼ cup cashews, crushed

2 teaspoons chopped fresh tarragon, separated

4 small skinless boneless chicken cutlets

Salt and freshly ground black pepper

1 teaspoon olive oil

1 tablespoon grass-fed butter

2 or 3 sprigs fresh tarragon

½ cup dry white wine

4 whole cloves garlic, roasted and skinned

2 tablespoons creamy canna-butter, plus ½ stick grass-fed butter

2 cups cremini and baby bella mushrooms (mixed), sliced ¼ inch thick

1   Heat small nonstick skillet over medium heat. Add the 3 cloves chopped garlic and chopped cashews; toast to lightly brown. When toasted, transfer to small bowl and mix in 1 teaspoon fresh chopped tarragon. Set aside.

2   Sprinkle the chicken with salt and pepper.

3   In a large preheated skillet, add the olive oil and grass-fed butter over medium-high heat. Spread around to mix evenly.

4   Add 2 or 3 sprigs of tarragon and sauté for 1 to 2 minutes till butter is fragrant. Add the chicken and cook until browned and cooked through, 3 to 4 minutes per side. Transfer the chicken to a plate and discard tarragon sprigs (do not clean skillet).

2 teaspoons Dijon mustard

½ cup chicken broth

½ cup half-and-half

Cornstarch slurry (mix 2 tablespoons cornstarch into 1 cup cold water)

5   Deglaze the skillet with a splash of wine. Add the 4 whole roasted garlic cloves and rest of wine. Cook until reduced by about half, mashing garlic with fork, about 1 minute. Add the canna-butter mixture and incorporate. Add the mushrooms, salt, pepper, and the remaining 1 teaspoon chopped tarragon. Sauté for 2 to 3 minutes until mushrooms are lightly browned. Add the Dijon mustard and chicken broth and simmer for 2 minutes. Add the half-and-half and continue to simmer. Slowly add the cornstarch slurry to the sauce, until it reaches your desired consistency. Add salt and pepper to taste.

6   Return the chicken to skillet. Simmer for 1 to 2 minutes on each side. Transfer chicken pieces to serving platter, spoon sauce over each piece, and sprinkle with crushed garlic-cashew mixture.

Approximate dose per serving is based on infusing 5 grams of cured/dried/decarbed cannabis into 1⅓ sticks of butter.

FREAKY FISH TACOS WITH LIME-CHIPOTLE CANNA-AIOLI

Fish tacos are a perfect dinner party meal. Not only are these really tasty (and authentic), but they have the potential to knock your socks off if you eat more than two. There is also something really rewarding about making your own salsa, so I included my cucumber-avocado salsa in this recipe for you. It's the perfect complement to this dish.

SERVINGS
8
tacos

PREP TIME
30
minutes

COOK TIME
30
minutes

APPROXIMATE
THC PER
SERVING*

10%: 3.8 mg

15%: 5.7 mg

20%: 7.6 mg

½ red onion, diced

½ cucumber, diced

1 avocado, diced

1 large tomato, diced

1 clove garlic, minced

¼ cup fresh cilantro leaves, chopped (reserve some for garnish)

1 jalapeño, stemmed and chopped

Red wine vinegar

1 teaspoon salt, plus more for seasoning

2 teaspoons lime juice

1 tablespoon canna-olive oil, plus 1 tablespoon extra-virgin olive oil

1 cup all-purpose or whole-wheat flour

1   Put the onion, cucumber, avocado, tomato, garlic, cilantro, and jalapeño in a small bowl. Pour in just enough red wine vinegar to cover well. Add a pinch of salt, the lime juice, and the canna-olive oil mixture. Set aside for at least 30 minutes.

2   In a large bowl, combine the flour, 1 teaspoon salt, garlic powder, chili powder, and cumin. Sift together well with a fork.

3   Season the fish with salt and pepper, then coat the fish with the flour mixture.

4   Preheat oven to 340°F.

5   At the same time, heat a large skillet over medium-high heat. Add 1 inch of olive oil. Gently fry the fish for 3 to 4 minutes, then turn over and cook for another 2 minutes. Remove the fish with a slotted spoon and drain on a plate lined with paper towels. Set aside.

½ teaspoon garlic powder

1⅓ teaspoons ancho chili powder

½ teaspoon ground cumin

1 pound flaky white fish (such as mahi-mahi or cod), cut into 4 pieces

Freshly ground black pepper

Olive oil for frying

8 fresh corn tortillas

1 cup shredded cabbage (use a mixture of red and green)

Lime-Chipotle Canna-Aioli (page 54)

2 limes, cut into quarters

6   Stack the tortillas, separating each with a slightly dampened sheet of paper towel. Wrap in foil. Heat in the oven for 5 minutes.

7   Top each tortilla with a pinch of shredded cabbage and some of the cooked fish, then, using a slotted spoon, top each one with the cucumber-avocado salsa. Garnish with Lime-Chipotle Canna-Aioli (page 54), a lime wedge, and cilantro. Dig in!

Approximate dose per serving is based on infusing 5 grams of cured/dried/decarbed cannabis into 5 ounces of oil.

Freaky Fish Tacos with Lime-Chipotle
Canna-Aioli, page 186

HOLIDAY CANNA-HAM

For some of us, it wouldn't be a proper holiday without a holiday ham, and this recipe is sure to deliver some extra holiday cheer.

1 (8- to 9-pound) boneless, precooked ham

½-inch finger of fresh ginger, peeled and sliced in half

1 teaspoon whole peppercorns

Pinch of ground nutmeg

Pinch of ground allspice

1 bay leaf, crushed

2 tablespoons melted canna-butter, plus 2 tablespoons melted unsalted grass-fed butter

½ cup brown sugar

½ cup dark cherry or maple syrup

1 teaspoon Dijon mustard

Pinch of salt

Cheesecloth

Kitchen string

40 whole cloves

1   Cook the ham according to the package directions and remove 30 minutes before it's done. Let it cool for 20 minutes.

2   In a Pyrex measuring cup, add ginger, peppercorns, nutmeg, allspice, and bay leaf. Add the canna-butter mixture and lower the Pyrex measuring cup into a pan of warm water that comes up to the line formed by the butter and spice mixture. This will infuse the flavors of the spices into your butter. Let it steep this way for 20 minutes.

3   In a medium saucepan, combine the brown sugar, cherry or maple syrup, mustard, and salt. Bring to a boil, stirring continuously. Stir and boil for 2 minutes, then set aside.

4   Score the ham in a "chessboard" pattern, cutting the horizontal lines about *3 inches* deep and the vertical lines about *½ inch* deep.

5   Strain the butter through the cheesecloth or a fine strainer into a clean measuring cup (or you can use a French press).

6   Use your fingers to gently open the vertical cuts in the ham, then evenly drizzle the canna-butter mixture into each vertical crevice. Tie the ham back together with kitchen twine.

7   Preheat oven to 340ºF. Using a brush, paint the glaze over the prepared ham. Place a whole clove in the center crosshatch of each square on the ham. Bake uncovered for 25 to 30 minutes, until the ham is beautifully caramelized. Voilà!

SERVINGS
10

PREP TIME
45
minutes

COOK TIME
1–1½
hours

APPROXIMATE
THC PER
SERVING*

10%: 4.6 mg

15%: 6.8 mg

20%: 9.2 mg

Approximate dose per serving is based on infusing 5 grams of cured/dried/decarbed cannabis into 1⅓ sticks of butter.

INFUSED LEMON-TARRAGON HALIBUT

This fish is flaky, flavorful, and buttery! Lemon and tarragon complement the lightly herbaceous flavor of the canna-butter and the subtle flavor of the fish. Serve with a slice or two of French bread to soak up all the goodness left on your plate.

Salt and freshly ground black pepper

4 halibut steaks, skin removed

1 teaspoon olive oil

1 tablespoon grass-fed butter

½ Spanish onion, chopped

4 sprigs tarragon

1 tablespoon creamy canna-butter, plus 1 tablespoon salted grass-fed butter

4 teaspoons fresh lemon juice

¼ cup chopped tarragon

¼ cup white wine

Toasted Almond & Garlic crumble (see sidebar, page 193)

1   Preheat a nonstick skillet over medium heat.

2   Salt and pepper both sides of the halibut steaks.

3   Melt 1 teaspoon olive oil and 1 tablespoon grass-fed butter together in the pan.

4   When the butter is completely melted and stops foaming, add the chopped onion and a pinch of salt. Sauté until onion is translucent.

5   Push the onion to the outer edge of the pan, leaving a bare landing spot for the fish. Strategically place 4 tarragon sprigs and position a fish fillet on top of each sprig.

6   Let the fish cook for about 2 minutes, then cover and cook over medium heat for another 3 to 5 minutes to allow the fish to steam through.

7   Remove the lid and carefully turn each steak. Drizzle with the canna-butter mixture, and cook uncovered for 4 more minutes. Remove the fish to a plate to rest for 10 minutes while you finish the sauce.

recipe continues

8   Add the lemon juice and chopped tarragon to the onion.

9   Add the wine and deglaze the pan by loosening up any bits that cling to the bottom. Keep the heat on medium and reduce the liquid in the pan until it thickens enough to coat the back of a spoon.

10   Plate the fish and drizzle each fillet with a little wine sauce. Sprinkle with Toasted Almond & Garlic Crumble, and serve!

Approximate dose per serving is based on infusing 5 grams of cured/dried/decarbed cannabis into 1⅓ sticks of butter.

Toasted Almond & Garlic Crumble (optional)

½ cup raw slivered almonds, slightly broken

4 cloves garlic, chopped

1 teaspoon olive oil

Sea salt

1   In a small bowl, mix the almonds and garlic with olive oil and dash of salt.

2   Spread evenly on a small pan and roast at 325°F for 25-30 minutes, until toasted and browned. Remove, let cool, and sprinkle over fish before serving.

TERIYAKI-GLAZED SALMON WITH GARLIC CANNA-AIOLI

The 1 hour marinade time boosts the flavor of the salmon, allowing the full flavor of the Asian-inspired sauce to soak in.

SERVINGS
4

PREP TIME
20
minutes

COOK TIME
25
minutes

IDLE TIME
1
hour

APPROXIMATE THC PER SERVING*

10%: 3.8 mg

15%: 5.7 mg

20%: 7.6 mg

*Approximate dose per serving is based on infusing 5 grams of cured/dried/decarbed cannabis into 5 ounces of oil for the canna-aioli.

FOR THE FISH

2 tablespoons rice vinegar

½ cup brown sugar, packed

½ tablespoon soy sauce

2 cloves garlic, minced

½ teaspoon ground ginger

½ teaspoon ground mace

½ tablespoon sesame oil

¾ cup water

2 tablespoons cornstarch

4 salmon fillets

FOR THE SPICY PEANUT GARLIC SAUCE

4 tablespoons Garlic Canna-Aioli (page 52, prepared without the dill)

2 tablespoons honey

1 to 2 tablespoons chili garlic sauce (Sambal)

Toasted Peanuts & Garlic (see sidebar, page 117)

PREPARE THE FISH

1   In a small saucepot, whisk the rice vinegar, brown sugar, soy sauce, garlic, ground ginger, ground mace, and sesame oil. Add ½ cup water and stir well. Bring to a boil.

2   Meanwhile, make a slurry by mixing the cornstarch into ¼ cup water. Lower the heat to medium and slowly mix in the slurry. Mix until the sauce sticks to the back of a spoon. Let cool.

3   Lightly grease a baking dish or spray it with cooking spray. Coat the bottom of the pan with half of the cooled teriyaki glaze. Place the salmon fillets in the prepared baking dish on top of the glaze. Paint the remaining teriyaki glaze over the salmon, letting it drip over and around the fish fillets. Cover with plastic wrap and marinate in the refrigerator for 1 hour.

PREPARE THE SPICY PEANUT GARLIC SAUCE

4   To make the sauce, whisk together the canna-aioli, honey, chili garlic sauce, and Toasted Peanuts & Garlic. Set aside.

5   Preheat oven to 400°F.

6   Remove plastic wrap from the salmon dish and bake for 20 to 25 minutes, until flaky and moist. Serve with spicy peanut garlic sauce.

WHACKY SHRIMP SCAMPI

In this "whacky" take on an Italian classic, the zesty, garlicky scampi is perfected with broiled shrimp in a simple but scrumptious dish.

1 box (16 ounces) angel-hair pasta

1 pound shrimp, peeled and deveined

Salt and freshly ground black pepper

2 tablespoons grass-fed butter

2 tablespoons olive oil

2 small shallots, sliced

4 garlic cloves, minced

½ teaspoon dried marjoram

½ teaspoon dried basil

¼ cup vermouth

2 teaspoons lemon juice

2 teaspoons canna-butter, plus 3 tablespoons grass-fed butter, melted

1 teaspoon lemon zest

2 tablespoons fresh parsley, roughly chopped

1   Boil the pasta according to directions in salted water until al dente (cooked yet firm), usually about 8 minutes.

2   Preheat oven to broil. Season the shrimp with salt and pepper, and set aside.

3   In a large skillet, melt the 2 tablespoons of grass-fed butter into the 2 tablespoons olive oil. Add shallots and sauté until translucent. Add garlic and cook until fragrant, about 1 minute. Add the shrimp and sprinkle with dried marjoram and basil.

4   Cook shrimp for 1 minute, turn, and cook for 2 more minutes until pink. Remove the shrimp from the skillet using tongs and place them on a baking pan. Broil for 2 minutes until nicely charred on the outside. Remove from the oven and let rest.

5   While the shrimp are broiling, deglaze the pan with vermouth by scraping up any bits clinging to the bottom of the pan. Add the lemon juice and canna-butter mixture and whisk until the sauce is smooth and silky. Bring sauce to a simmer and immediately add in the broiled shrimp and toss. Add the lemon zest and test for seasoning. Add salt and black pepper, if necessary.

6   Garnish with fresh parsley, and serve immediately over pasta.

SERVINGS

4

(5 or 6 shrimp per serving)

PREP TIME

25

minutes

COOK TIME

10

minutes

APPROXIMATE THC PER SERVING*

10%: 3.8 mg

15%: 6.4 mg

20%: 7.6 mg

*Approximate dose per serving is based on infusing 5 grams of cured/dried/decarbed cannabis into 1⅓ sticks of butter.

HAZY THAI COCONUT CURRY CHICKEN

I learned the basics of this recipe when I was in Thailand a few years ago. It's authentic, insanely delicious, and now it's medicinal, too! There is something about the flavors of coconut milk and curry with a hint of cannabis that puts this dish over the top.

2 tablespoons extra-virgin coconut oil

1 white onion, diced

1 cup toasted cashews

6 skinless boneless chicken cutlets, cut into 1-inch pieces

½ cup cornstarch

3 cloves garlic, minced

1 green bell pepper, diced

1 red bell pepper, diced

1½ cups (or one 15-ounce can) organic unsweetened coconut milk

1 teaspoon salt, plus more to taste

1 teaspoon red pepper flakes

1 teaspoon red curry powder

1½ cups jasmine rice

1 tablespoon extra-virgin canna–coconut oil, plus 3 tablespoons extra-virgin coconut oil

Shredded unsweetened coconut for garnish

1 Preheat a large Dutch oven and add 2 tablespoons of coconut oil. Add the onion and cashews and sauté until the onion is translucent. Coat the chicken with the cornstarch and add to the pan.

2 Add the garlic, green pepper, and red pepper and continue to sauté for 2 minutes. Add the coconut milk, salt, red pepper flakes, and curry powder. Reduce heat to low. Cover and cook for 20 minutes, lifting the lid to stir occasionally.

3 Prepare jasmine rice according to package instructions.

4 Add the canna–coconut oil mixture to the chicken, cover, and cook for 10 more minutes.

5 Sprinkle with shredded coconut, and serve over jasmine rice.

Approximate dose per serving is based on infusing 5 grams of cured/dried/decarbed cannabis into 5 ounces of oil.

SERVINGS
6

PREP TIME
15
minutes

COOK TIME
30
minutes

APPROXIMATE THC PER SERVING*

10%: 5 mg

15%: 7.6 mg

20%: 10 mg

CANNA-COCONUT SHRIMP

Bubba Gump said, "You can barbecue it, boil it, broil it, bake it, sauté it. There's shrimp kebabs, shrimp creole, shrimp gumbo. Pan-fried, deep-fried, stir-fried. There's pineapple shrimp, lemon shrimp, coconut shrimp, pepper shrimp, shrimp soup, shrimp stew, shrimp salad, shrimp and potatoes, shrimp burger, shrimp sandwich. That, that's about it." He forgot one thing—you can infuse it! And there is nothing like cannabis-infused coconut shrimp—with cannabis-infused dipping sauce. If only Bubba knew!

FOR THE SHRIMP

2 cups shredded coconut

1 egg white

⅔ cup ginger beer

½ cup all-purpose flour

1½ teaspoons baking powder

1 teaspoon salt

½ teaspoon freshly ground black pepper

1 pound jumbo shrimp, tail on, peeled and deveined (about 24)

½ teaspoon lemon zest

2 cups extra-virgin coconut oil

1 teaspoon extra-virgin canna–coconut oil, plus 2 tablespoons extra-virgin coconut oil

1   Line a baking sheet with parchment paper. Sprinkle 1 cup of shredded coconut on the paper.

2   Mix the egg white, a pinch of coconut flakes, ginger beer, flour, baking powder, salt, and pepper in a medium shallow bowl. Dip the shrimp in the batter and place on the prepared baking sheet. Sprinkle the lemon zest over shrimp, cover, and refrigerate.

3   Preheat a frying pan on medium-high and add the extra-virgin coconut oil. Hold the shrimp by the tail, and dredge in the remaining coconut. Fry shrimp for 1 to 1½ minutes on each side until golden brown. Using tongs, remove shrimp to brown paper or paper towels to drain.

4   Drizzle with the canna–coconut oil mixture and serve with canna-dipping sauce.

recipe continues

SERVINGS
4
(5 or 6 shrimp per serving)

PREP TIME
25
minutes

COOK TIME
3
minutes

APPROXIMATE THC PER SERVING (INCLUDES DIPPING SAUCE)*

10%: 3.6 mg
15%; 6 mg
20%: 7.8 mg

1 tablespoon melted
creamy canna-butter,
plus 2 tablespoons
grass-fed butter

⅓ cup honey

¼ cup horseradish
mustard

1 teaspoon chili garlic
sauce (Sambal)
(optional, for spice)

2 teaspoons yellow curry
powder

1 teaspoon orange juice

2 teaspoons fresh lemon
juice

PREPARE THE DIPPING SAUCE

5   In small bowl, whisk together the canna-butter mixture, honey, mustard, and chili garlic sauce. Sprinkle in the curry powder and whisk well. Slowly add the orange juice and lemon juice and continue to whisk until creamy.

Approximate dose per serving (shrimp) is based on infusing 5 grams of cured/dried/decarbed cannabis into 5 ounces of oil. Approximate dose per serving (dipping sauce) is based on infusing 5 grams of cured/dried/decarbed cannabis into 1⅓ sticks of butter.

SALTED CANNA-CAPER SALMON OVER FARFALLE WITH TOASTED CAPERS

Salmon and capers are an unusual pairing with cannabis–but boy is it tasty. While great served hot for dinner, it's also a big hit when served cold for Sunday brunch.

SERVINGS
6

PREP TIME
40
minutes

COOK TIME
15–20
minutes

APPROXIMATE THC PER SERVING*

10%: 5 mg

15%: 7.6 mg

20%: 10 mg

*Approximate dose per serving is based on infusing 5 grams of cured/dried/decarbed cannabis into 5 ounces of oil.

1 pound farfalle pasta

¼ cup olive oil, plus 1 tablespoon

2 tablespoons salted capers, lightly rinsed (you want to keep some of the salt on them) and dried

1 tablespoon Dijon mustard

1 teaspoon lemon zest

1 tablespoon canna–olive oil, plus 3 tablespoons extra-virgin olive oil

2-pound wild salmon fillet

2 sprigs fresh dill, minced

1   Boil the pasta according to package directions until al dente (cooked yet firm), 8 to 9 minutes. Drain, rinse, and toss in 1 tablespoon olive oil. Set aside.

2   Preheat a medium skillet and add the remaining olive oil. Add the capers to the hot oil and fry for about 1 minute until the capers puff up a little. Using a slotted spoon, remove the capers to a plate lined with paper towels.

3   Reserve the salted caper oil and mix with the Dijon mustard, lemon zest, and canna-olive oil mixture.

4   Preheat a grill to medium-high.

5   Brush the bottom side of the salmon with olive oil. Brush the top with the salted canna-caper oil. (You might need to reserve some of this to baste with while you're grilling.)

6   Place the salmon fillet, skin side down, in the center of the grill and cook for 7 to 8 minutes, until you start to see fatty white protein coming out of the sides and top. The flesh should be moist and flaky. Remove from the grill, put on a platter over the farfalle, sprinkle with dill, and garnish with toasted capers before serving.

METERSPAÄTZ

I created this tasty recipe one night while at Wirtshaus, a German restaurant in L.A., with Chef André Lujan. If you like schnitzel and beer, you'll love this dish. It's a thin chicken cutlet dredged in lemon butter and cranberry sauce, breaded with Hefeweizen beer-tarragon batter and lightly fried, then topped with canna-garlic-mustard seed aioli to finish. You might be wondering where the name Meterspaätz came from. After André and I met up at the restaurant, I asked him if he'd parked in a meter spot. Always one to be thinking about food, he answered, "Meterspaätz? I didn't see that on the menu." With that, the dish made its way into the book—and hopefully onto your dinner table!

SERVINGS
4

PREP TIME
40
minutes

COOK TIME
15–20
minutes

APPROXIMATE
THC PER
SERVING*

10%: 5 mg

15%: 7.6 mg

20%: 10 mg

FOR THE CHICKEN

1 teaspoon lemon juice

½ cup grass-fed butter, melted

4 chicken cutlets

Salt and black pepper

1 cup all-purpose flour plus ¼ cup for dusting

½ cup cranberry sauce

1 teaspoon garlic powder

½ teaspoon white pepper

2 eggs

1¼ cups Hefeweizen beer

1 teaspoon tarragon, minced

1 teaspoon lemon zest

Olive oil for frying

PREPARE THE CHICKEN

1   In a large bowl, mix the lemon juice with melted butter.

2   Pound the chicken until evenly flat and very thin, about ⅛ inch thick. Sprinkle the cutlets with salt and pepper and dust both sides with flour. Brush both sides of each cutlet with the cranberry sauce.

3   In a large bowl, mix together the 1 cup flour, garlic powder, ½ teaspoon salt, and ½ teaspoon white pepper.

4   In a separate bowl, mix the eggs, beer, and tarragon.

5   Slowly add the flour mixture to the beer mixture to create a batter (the batter will be thin). Add the lemon zest and mix well.

6   Preheat a large skillet over medium-high heat and add the olive oil. Dip the cutlets into the lemon butter and then into the batter. Fry until golden brown on both sides. Hold in a warm oven (150° to 200°F) while you finish the aioli.

FOR THE AIOLI

1 tablespoon dried
  mustard seeds

2 large egg yolks

4 teaspoons fresh lemon
  juice

1 teaspoon Dijon mustard

2 teaspoons extra-light
  canna–olive oil, plus 5
  tablespoons light olive
  oil

2 chives, minced fine

Sea salt

PREPARE THE AIOLI

7   Toast mustard seeds in a saucepan over medium heat for about 5 minutes until lightly browned and fragrant. If they start to pop, that's a sign that they're toasted. Pull them from the heat and let sit at room temperature.

8   Make sure all of the following ingredients and utensils are at room temperature.

9   In medium bowl, whisk egg yolks, lemon juice, and Dijon mustard.

10   Slowly drizzle the canna–olive oil mixture into the egg yolk mixture and whisk until all the oils are incorporated and aioli is smooth and creamy. If the oil separates, have no fear. Stop adding the oil and keep whisking until it's incorporated.

11   Whisk in the toasted mustard seeds, chives, and a pinch or two of sea salt, until smooth and creamy.

12   Serve alongside the warm Meterspaätz.

Approximate dose per serving is based on infusing 5 grams of cured/dried/decarbed cannabis into 5 ounces of oil.

Sweet Potato Gnocchi, page 215

CHAPTER NO. 8

Pastas & Breads

FETTUCCINE ALFREDO

Another fan favorite! This delicious, creamy, cheesy Italian classic with a medicinal twist will have you making it once a week. The balance of salty and creamy and umami hits just the right note.

SERVINGS
6

PREP TIME
20
minutes

COOK TIME
10
minutes

APPROXIMATE
THC PER
SERVING*
10%: 3.8 mg
15%: 5.7 mg
20%: 7.6 mg

1 pound fettuccine pasta

1½ cups milk

¼ cup chicken stock, room temperature

2 tablespoons grass-fed butter

1 tablespoon olive oil

1 tablespoon canna-butter

1 clove fresh garlic, minced or pressed

¼ cup all-purpose flour

1 cup freshly grated Parmesan cheese

½ teaspoon salt, plus more to taste

½ teaspoon freshly ground black pepper, plus more to taste

¼ teaspoon freshly grated nutmeg

2 chives, minced

1   Boil pasta according to directions until al dente (cooked yet firm), usually 8 to 9 minutes.

2   In a measuring cup combine the milk and chicken stock. Preheat a medium saucepot on low and add grass-fed butter and oil. Add the canna-butter and let it all melt together. Add the garlic, then mix in the flour a little at a time until a paste forms.

3   Slowly add the milk-stock mixture to the paste and stir until creamy, about 4 to 5 minutes. Next, slowly add in the Parmesan cheese. Continue to stir every minute or so until the cheese is melted and incorporated. Add the salt and pepper and stir. Taste and adjust seasonings, as necessary.

4   Drain the pasta, saving a bit of the cooking water to thin the sauce if necessary.

5   Put the drained pasta and sauce together in the pot and add a bit of pasta cooking water. Cook for 1 to 2 minutes, until the sauce is a silky consistency and coats the pasta.

6   Transfer to a serving bowl and garnish with the chives.

Approximate dose per serving is based on infusing 5 grams of cured/dried/decarbed cannabis into 1⅓ sticks of butter.

POPPIN' BASIL & PINE NUT CHICKEN ORECCHIETTE

Orecchiette, the name of this pasta, comes from its shape, which resembles a small ear. This fun-shaped pasta gets even better when you throw some protein, herbs, and toasted pine nuts into the mix—and, of course, some canna–olive oil.

1 pound orecchiette pasta

4 boneless, skinless chicken breasts, pounded thin

Salt and pepper

1 cup all-purpose flour

½ cup pine nuts

2 tablespoons olive oil, plus more for sautéing

1 tablespoon grass-fed butter

1 small sweet onion, halved and sliced thin

4 cloves garlic, slivered

½ cup basil leaves

1 teaspoon lemon zest

1 tablespoon extra-virgin canna–olive oil, plus 3 tablespoons extra-virgin olive oil

1   Boil the pasta according to package directions until al dente (cooked yet firm), drain, and set aside.

2   Salt and pepper the chicken and coat with flour.

3   Preheat a large skillet and toast the pine nuts. Shake the pan gently until lightly browned and fragrant, 2 to 4 minutes. Remove to a small plate to let cool.

4   Add the olive oil and butter to the pan, then add the onion, garlic, and a dash of salt and sauté until golden brown. Next, add the basil and lemon zest, then remove from the heat. Continue to stir about 2 minutes until the basil is wilted but still bright green.

5   Remove the onion-garlic-basil mixture from the pan with a slotted spoon and set aside.

6   Add a little more olive oil to coat the bottom of the pan. Place chicken in the same skillet and cook until lightly browned and cooked through, 3 to 4 minutes on each side.

7   Transfer the cooked pasta to a large pot and drizzle with canna–olive oil. Add the onion mixture and toss.

8   Serve the chicken over the orecchiette and sprinkle with pine nuts to finish.

SERVINGS
6

PREP TIME
30
minutes

COOK TIME
45
minutes

APPROXIMATE THC PER SERVING*

10%: 5 mg

15%: 7.6 mg

20%: 10 mg

*Approximate dose per serving is based on infusing 5 grams of cured/dried/decarbed cannabis into 5 ounces of oil.

WHACKY MAC & CHEESE

This is my favorite comfort food of all time, and this version is creamy and packed with flavor. The lobster version (page 210) also happens to be one of my most asked-for dishes. When mac and cheese is already a favorite, it can only get better with cannabis—and lobster!

1-pound box ziti rigati or large elbow macaroni

2 cups milk

½ teaspoon Dijon mustard

¼ cup chicken stock, room temperature

3 tablespoons grass-fed butter

1 tablespoon olive oil

1 tablespoon canna-butter, plus 1 tablespoon salted grass-fed butter

¼ cup all-purpose flour

½ pound Emmenthaler Swiss cheese, diced into ½-inch cubes

¼ pound yellow sharp cheddar cheese, diced into ½-inch cubes

½ teaspoon salt

½ teaspoon black pepper

½ teaspoon garlic powder

1 teaspoon onion powder

White truffle oil (optional)

1   Boil the pasta according to package directions until al dente (cooked yet firm), usually 8 to 9 minutes.

2   In a measuring cup, combine the milk, Dijon mustard, and chicken stock.

3   Over medium heat, melt the grass-fed butter and olive oil. Lower the heat and melt in the canna-butter mixture. Mix in the flour, 1 teaspoon at a time, until you form a paste. Slowly add the milk mixture to the paste and stir until creamy, about 4 to 5 minutes. Add in the cheese and continue to stir every minute or so until it melts. Add the salt, pepper, garlic powder, and onion powder. Stir well to combine. Lower the heat and let the sauce simmer until it starts to bubble and look thick. Immediately remove from the heat and stir.

4   Preheat oven to 340°F and grease a large 9-by-13-inch baking dish.

5   Drain the pasta and return it to the pot. Mix three-quarters of the sauce into the pasta. Transfer to the prepared baking dish and cover with the rest of the sauce. Bake for 20 minutes and then raise the oven temperature to broil. Watch carefully as you broil for 5 to 7 minutes until the top is golden brown.

6   Remove from the oven, sprinkle with truffle oil (optional), and serve.

Approximate dose per serving is based on infusing 5 grams of cured/dried/decarbed cannabis into 1⅓ sticks of butter.

Lobster-Canna Mac & Cheese

2 teaspoons Meyer lemon juice

1 pound fresh lobster meat, cooked, cut into ½-inch to 1-inch chunks

Salt and freshly ground black pepper

¼ cup all-purpose flour

1 tablespoon grass-fed butter

1 tablespoon olive oil

2 medium shallots, sliced

1 clove garlic, minced

1   Sprinkle Meyer lemon juice over the lobster and toss with some salt and pepper. Dredge the lobster bits in flour and set aside.

2   Preheat a medium saucepot on medium-high and add the grass-fed butter and oil. Add the shallots and sauté until translucent. Add the lobster and garlic. Raise the heat. Sear the lobster bits until the coating and shallots are lightly browned. With a slotted spoon, remove the lobster and shallots and mix in with the pasta.

CANNA-GARLIC KNOTS

Calling all bread bakers and non-bread bakers alike—it's time to try your hand at garlic knots! These are over-the-top flavorful and addictive, the way good munchies should be.

1 cup warm water (105° to 110°F)

1 envelope active dry yeast

1 teaspoon honey

3 tablespoons canna-olive oil, plus 3 tablespoons extra-virgin olive oil

2 teaspoons dried basil

1 teaspoon salt

3 cups bread flour or high-gluten flour

¼ cup extra-virgin olive oil

6 cloves garlic, minced

2 teaspoons Italian parsley, chopped fine

¼ cup Parmesan cheese, grated

Dried oregano

1   Combine the water, yeast, honey, and 1 tablespoon of the canna-olive oil mixture. Let sit about 5 minutes until the yeast foams.

2   Mix the dried basil and salt into the flour.

3   Add 1½ cups of the flour to the yeast mixture and mix by hand until it's incorporated and the dough is smooth. Continue adding flour, ¼ cup at a time, working the dough until it is smooth and slightly sticky. Knead on a lightly floured surface until smooth and barely sticky, 4 to 5 minutes.

4   Oil a large mixing bowl with 1 tablespoon of canna-olive oil mixture. Place the dough in the bowl, turning to coat with the oil. Cover with plastic wrap and set in a warm place for 1½ to 2 hours until dough doubles in size.

5   Once the dough has doubled in size, roll it out on a floured surface into a large rectangle. Slice the rectangle in half and then cut each side into 12 equal strips. Roll each strip into a "rope" and then tie each rope into a simple knot. Place knots on a parchment paper-lined baking sheet and let rest in a warm spot for about 1 hour, until they look plump and doubled in size. Meanwhile, preheat oven to 350°F.

SERVINGS
24
knots

PREP TIME
2
hours and 15 minutes

COOK TIME
20
minutes

IDLE TIME
2½–3
hours

APPROXIMATE THC PER SERVING*

10%: 3.8 mg

15%: 5.7 mg

20%: 7.6 mg

recipe continues

6　Bake knots for 20 to 25 minutes until they are golden brown. Remove and let cool on the baking sheet. Add the extra-virgin olive oil to a small saucepan over low heat and add the garlic. Cook gently until the garlic becomes fragrant, about 5 minutes. Remove to a large bowl, along with the remaining canna-olive oil, parsley, Parmesan cheese, and a pinch or two of oregano.

7　Toss the baked garlic knots in the mixture of canna-olive oil, garlic, and Parmesan, and serve.

Approximate dose per serving is based on infusing 5 grams of cured/dried/decarbed cannabis into 5 ounces of oil.

SWEET POTATO GNOCCHI WITH LEMON PESTO

Homemade gnocchi? No way, you say! But this recipe is really fun and simple, so don't let it scare you. It's not your typical sweet potato gnocchi recipe either (then again, nothing in this book is typical). The combination of sweet potato gnocchi with savory canna-pesto makes for a fresh and tasty surprise.

SERVINGS

6

PREP TIME

1

hour

COOK TIME

15

minutes

APPROXIMATE THC PER SERVING*

10%: 5 mg

15%: 7.6 mg

20%: 10 mg

FOR THE GNOCCHI

½ cup ricotta cheese

3 sweet potatoes

1 teaspoon brown sugar

¼ teaspoon cinnamon

½ teaspoon nutmeg

2 cups whole-wheat flour

FOR THE PESTO

1 cup basil

1 garlic clove

¼ cup Parmesan, grated

¼ cup hazelnuts, toasted

1 tablespoon extra-virgin canna–olive oil, plus 3 tablespoons extra-virgin olive oil

1 teaspoon lemon zest

PREPARE THE GNOCCHI

1   Preheat oven to 425°F.

2   Drain the ricotta cheese. You want it as dry as possible.

3   Poke the potatoes with a fork to allow steam to escape while cooking. Place the potatoes on top of aluminum foil and bake for 45 minutes to 1 hour (depending on center thickness). When done, turn off the oven and let sit for 20 minutes. Slice and let cool.

4   Scoop the flesh from the sweet potatoes into a large bowl and mix in the ricotta cheese. Add the sugar, cinnamon, and nutmeg. Work the flour into this mixture until you have a somewhat firm, nonsticky dough.

5   Bring a large pot of salted water to a boil. Divide dough into 4 even pieces and roll into 1-inch-thick ropes. Cut each rope into 1-inch pieces. Gently press the back of a fork into each piece to make an imprint. Drop the gnocchi into boiling water and cook for 3 minutes. Remove with slotted spoon and keep warm.

recipe continues

6   Combine the basil, garlic, Parmesan, and hazelnuts in a food processor. Pulse and slowly add the canna-olive oil mixture. Process until fully incorporated and smooth. Mix in the lemon zest by hand. Season with salt and pepper, and pour over gnocchi before serving.

Approximate dose per serving is based on infusing 5 grams of cured/dried/decarbed cannabis into 5 ounces of oil.

CANNA-PAN DE QUESO (GLUTEN-FREE)

Anyone who has been to the Rocking Horse in New York City knows how addicting these little cheesy bread balls can be. Once you try them infused with cannabis, you'll want to freeze a batch for regular snacking.

2½ cups yucca or tapioca starch (or you can substitute potato starch)

2 cups grated Asiago cheese

1 teaspoon baking powder

Pinch of salt

½ stick creamy canna-butter, plus ½ stick unsalted grass-fed butter, softened

2 large eggs

1 clove minced garlic

2 tablespoons milk

1   In a large bowl, combine yucca or tapioca starch, cheese, baking powder, and salt. Add in the butters, eggs, and minced garlic. Slowly add the milk as you mix the dough. Loosely cover dough and chill in refrigerator for 45 minutes.

2   Preheat oven to 340°F.

3   Using a small ice cream scoop to measure, create dough balls the size of golf balls. Place the dough balls on a cookie sheet lined with parchment paper and bake for 5 to 7 minutes, until golden. Turn on broiler to brown the tops for 1 to 1½ minutes, then serve.

Approximate dose per serving is based on infusing 5 grams of cured/dried/decarbed cannabis into 1⅓ sticks of butter.

SERVINGS
24
rolls

PREP TIME
10
minutes

COOK TIME
5–8
minutes

IDLE TIME
45
minutes

APPROXIMATE THC PER SERVING*

10%: 1.9 mg

15%: 2.8 mg

20%: 3.8 mg

TRICOLOR PASTA WITH CANNA-OIL VINAIGRETTE

This dish is perfect for a lazy-day picnic meal, especially when you're looking to lounge around and stare at the shapes of the clouds.

SERVINGS
6

PREP TIME
20
minutes

COOK TIME
9
minutes

APPROXIMATE THC PER SERVING*
10%: 5 mg
15%: 7.6 mg
20%: 10 mg

FOR THE DRESSING

2 tablespoons fresh lemon juice

1 tablespoon balsamic vinegar

1 teaspoon finely minced garlic clove

1 tablespoon extra-virgin canna–olive oil, plus 2 tablespoons extra-virgin olive oil

½ teaspoon salt

FOR THE PASTA

1 pound curly pasta

1 pint multicolored cherry tomatoes or 4 heirloom tomatoes, halved

1 (15-ounce) can cannellini beans, drained

1 medium shallot, sliced thin

1½ cups fresh mozzarella, diced small

1 tablespoon extra-virgin olive oil

½ cup basil, as chiffonade (see sidebar)

Maldon sea salt and coarsely ground black pepper

¼ cup freshly grated Parmesan cheese

PREPARE THE DRESSING

1   Mix together the dressing ingredients and set aside.

PREPARE THE PASTA

2   Boil the pasta according to the package directions until al dente (cooked yet firm), 8 to 9 minutes.

3   Place the cherry tomatoes, beans, shallot, and mozzarella in a medium bowl. Toss with 1 tablespoon extra-virgin olive oil, three-quarters of the basil, Maldon sea salt, and pepper.

4   Drain the pasta and rinse in cold water.

5   Toss tomato mixture into the pasta. Drizzle with the canna-dressing and toss until evenly coated. Top with the reserved basil and freshly grated Parmesan, and serve.

Approximate dose per serving is based on infusing 5 grams of cured/dried/decarbed cannabis into 5 ounces of oil.

HOW TO CHIFFONADE

Stack a few leaves of the herb or leafy green vegetable you want to chiffonade and roll them up lengthwise into a "joint" shape. Slice your knife across the "joint" to create shreds of long, thin strips.

POPPIN' PITA CHIPS

This is another fun collaboration with Chef Adrian Hale that combines two recipes in one: Homemade Pita and Canna-Garlic-Infused Pita Chips. Note: It takes a lot of time to make the dough, but it's easy to do and worth the time involved. You'll need a pizza stone to make these properly.

SERVINGS
12

PREP TIME
14
hours

COOK TIME
5–25
minutes

IDLE TIME
3–4
hours, then 12
hours

APPROXIMATE
THC PER
SERVING*

10%:	2.5 mg
15%:	3.8 mg
20%:	5 mg

FOR THE HOMEMADE PITA

4 cups of warm filtered water

¼ cup olive oil

4½ cups all-purpose flour

4½ cups whole-wheat flour

¼ to ½ teaspoon instant yeast

2 tablespoons salt

FOR THE CANNA–GARLIC–INFUSED PITA CHIPS

6 cloves garlic, halved

1 tablespoon extra-virgin canna–olive oil, plus 3 tablespoons extra-virgin olive oil

Maldon sea salt

FOR THE HOMEMADE PITA

1   Mix the water and olive oil. Add both flours and the yeast. Mix with your hands until a "shaggy" dough forms. Cover with a kitchen towel and let it rest 35 to 40 minutes. Add salt to dough mixture and combine. Cover with the kitchen towel and let the dough rest again for 35 to 40 minutes.

2   Remove the kitchen towel, reach under the dough, and pull up the corners to fold the bottom of the dough over the top, turning the bowl a bit after each fold so that the whole round of dough is folded into itself. Cover and let rest for 30 minutes. Repeat this step six times.

3   Cover the bowl with a plate or plastic wrap and let it rest untouched for 12 hours.

4   Line a sheet pan with parchment paper and sprinkle with flour.

5   Lightly flour your hands and pull off a piece of dough about the size of a baseball. Re-cover the dough so it doesn't dry out. Shape the dough into a round puffy ball. Repeat until you have 12 to 18 puffy balls. Set aside the ones you want to bake now and freeze any you want to keep for later.

6   Place a pizza stone in the oven. Preheat oven to its highest setting, 500° to 550°F.

7   Sprinkle flour on a clean cutting board, flip dough balls on the board a couple of times to lightly flour both sides, then press the dough down with the palm of your hand to form and shape to the size you like. Throw the shaped pita dough directly onto the stone and bake until the loaves puff up, about 5 to 7 minutes.

8   Remove to a basket and serve warm.

FOR THE POPPIN' PITA CHIPS

9   Cut the pita through the air pocket and then cut each half into 1-inch pieces.

10 Preheat oven to 300°F.

11 Rub cut garlic on each pita piece and place on a parchment paper-lined baking sheet. Drizzle the canna-olive oil mixture over the chips. Bake for 20 minutes until chips are crisp and lightly browned. Sprinkle with Maldon sea salt, and serve with your favorite dip.

*Approximate dose per serving is based on infusing 5 grams of cured/dried/decarbed cannabis into 5 ounces of oil.

FANTASY FOCACCIA

I like to serve this as an appetizer at my dinner parties and challenge guests to pick out the cannabis flavor. In addition to the light crust, the abundance of herbs plays nicely with the canna-olive oil and makes this one of the best focaccias I've ever had. If you enjoy dough, cheese, and tomatoes, you'll love this.

1 packet active dry yeast

1 cup warm water (105° to 110°F)

1 teaspoon fresh oregano, chopped

1 teaspoon fresh thyme, chopped

¼ cup fresh basil, as chiffonade (see sidebar, page 218)

2 teaspoons minced garlic

1 tablespoon extra-virgin canna–olive oil, plus 3 tablespoons extra-virgin olive oil

1 teaspoon salt, plus a pinch

2¾ cups all-purpose flour

1 teaspoon white sugar

1 teaspoon dried oregano

3 tablespoons olive oil

1 cup Roma tomatoes, diced

4 tablespoons Parmesan cheese, grated

1½ cups mozzarella cheese, shredded

Coarsely ground black pepper

1   Mix the yeast and water in a small bowl. Let sit 5 to 10 minutes until the yeast foams.

2   In another small bowl, combine all the fresh oregano, thyme, and basil with 1 teaspoon garlic, the canna–olive oil mixture, and a pinch of salt. Set aside.

3   In a large bowl, stir together the flour, 1 teaspoon salt, sugar, dried oregano, and remaining minced garlic. Add the yeast mixture and 1 tablespoon of olive oil to dry ingredients and combine to create the dough. Turn out onto a lightly floured surface and knead until smooth and elastic, about 7 to 10 minutes.

4   Lightly oil a large bowl, place the dough in the bowl, and turn to coat with olive oil. Cover with a damp cloth and let rise in a warm place for 30 minutes.

5   Preheat oven to 425°F.

6   Punch the dough down, place on a greased baking sheet, and pat down into a ½-inch-thick rectangle. Make indentations with your fingertips in the dough about ½ inch apart. Prick dough with a fork. Brush the top with the remaining olive oil and bake for 10 minutes.

SERVINGS
8

PREP TIME
45
minutes

COOK TIME
15–17
minutes

IDLE TIME
30
minutes

APPROXIMATE THC PER SERVING*

10%: 3.8 mg

15%: 5.7 mg

20%: 7.6 mg

recipe continues

7 Reduce oven heat to 340°F.

8 Remove from the oven and brush freely with the remaining canna–olive oil mixture, then evenly sprinkle with herbs, Roma tomatoes, and Parmesan and mozzarella cheeses.

9 Sprinkle with freshly ground black pepper and bake for an additional 5 to 7 minutes, until lightly golden brown. Remove from the oven and serve once cooled.

Approximate dose per serving is based on infusing 5 grams of cured/dried/decarbed cannabis into 5 ounces of oil.

POPPY-LIME ZUCCHINI BREAD

There is something irresistible about this recipe that keeps my friends coming back for more. The texture is great and the bread is dense, sticky, and very tasty. As one friend put it (as an ode to Jon Stewart), it's like a "delicious fruitcake . . . on weed."

½ cup roasted salted pistachios, shelled and lightly crushed

2 tablespoons canna-coconut oil, plus 3 tablespoons coconut oil

¾ cup whole-wheat flour

¾ cup bread flour or high-gluten flour

½ teaspoon salt

½ teaspoon baking powder

½ teaspoon baking soda

½ teaspoon ground mace

¼ cup poppy seeds

2 medium eggs

¼ cup light coconut oil

2 teaspoons lime juice

2 teaspoon lime zest

1¼ cups raw cane sugar

1 cup grated zucchini

1   Preheat oven to 300°F.

2   In a small pan or baking tin mix crushed pistachios with 1 tablespoon of canna-coconut oil mixture. Roast for 12 to 15 minutes.

3   Turn the oven up to 325°F. Grease and flour a standard loaf pan (4 inches by 8 inches).

4   In a large bowl, sift the flours, salt, baking powder, baking soda, mace, and poppy seeds.

5   In a separate bowl, whisk the eggs, light coconut oil, remaining canna-coconut oil mixture, lime juice, lime zest, and sugar.

6   Add the flour mixture to egg-and-oil mixture. Stir in the zucchini and pistachios until well combined. Pour the batter into the loaf pan and bake for 1 hour or until tester inserted in the center comes out clean.

7   Cool for 30 minutes, then flip the bread out of pan, cut, and serve.

Approximate dose per serving is based on infusing 5 grams of cured/dried/decarbed cannabis into 5 ounces of oil.

SERVINGS

12

PREP TIME

30

minutes

COOK TIME

1

hour

APPROXIMATE THC PER SERVING*

10%: 5 mg

15%: 7.6 mg

20%: 10 mg

JALAPEÑO CORN BREAD

This flavor-packed corn bread is chock-full of creamy canna-butter, sweet onions, and peppers and could be a meal unto itself. It's incredibly tasty and moist, with just a little bit of "zing," exactly the way corn bread should be.

1 stick salted grass-fed butter, melted

3 cups all-purpose flour

1 cup yellow cornmeal

¼ cup sugar

2 tablespoons baking powder

2 teaspoons kosher salt

2 cups milk

3 extra-large eggs, lightly beaten

½ stick creamy canna-butter, melted, plus ½ stick grass-fed butter, melted

½ sweet onion, minced

½ red bell pepper, minced

2 fresh jalapeño peppers, seeded and minced

½ cup sweet corn, thoroughly drained

1 scallion, green parts only, minced

4 ounces pepper jack cheese

4 ounces chipotle cheddar, grated, divided

1   Preheat oven to 340°F.

2   Grease a 9-by-13-inch baking pan with some of the melted grass-fed butter.

3   In a large bowl, combine the flour, cornmeal, sugar, baking powder, and salt.

4   In a separate bowl, mix together the milk, eggs, melted canna-butter mixture, and remaining grass-fed butter.

5   Add the dry ingredients to the wet ingredients and combine until only small lumps are visible.

6   Mix in the minced onion, red pepper, jalapeños, corn, and scallion. Add the cheeses and gently incorporate. Allow the mixture to sit at room temperature for 20 minutes.

7   Pour the batter into the greased baking pan and bake for 33 to 38 minutes, until toothpick comes out clean. Let cool, cut into 12 equal pieces, and serve.

Approximate dose per serving is based on infusing 5 grams of cured/dried/decarbed cannabis into 1⅓ sticks of butter.

SERVINGS
12

PREP TIME
30
minutes

COOK TIME
33–38
minutes

APPROXIMATE THC PER SERVING*

10%: 3.8 mg

15%: 5.7 mg

20%: 7.6 mg

The Double-Whammy
Ice Cream Sandwich,
page 246

CHAPTER NO. 9

Sweets & Snacks

CANNA-APPLE ROSES & CANNA-APPLE ROSE PARTY TOWER

Canna-Apple Roses are flaky, crispy, and gorgeous and present a unique take on apple pie. The cardamom and rose water are elegant additions to a recipe that is sure to impress guests. And for an awesomely beautiful party tower, you can quadruple the recipe and build a tower by stacking the apple roses like a pyramid and using melted Caramel Sauce (page 253) poured over the top of each one to hold the ones above in place. If you use paper muffin cups, be sure to remove them before stacking.

SERVINGS
12

PREP TIME
25
minutes

COOK TIME
18–20
minutes

IDLE TIME
1
hour

APPROXIMATE THC PER SERVING*

10%: 3.8 mg

15%: 5.7 mg

20%: 7.6 mg

FOR THE CANNA PASTRY DOUGH

2 cups all-purpose flour

¾ teaspoon salt

½ stick creamy canna-butter, cut into 4 pats

2 sticks cold grass-fed butter, diced into ¼-inch cubes

½ cup cold water

PREPARE THE CANNA PASTRY DOUGH

1 Put the flour and salt in a food processor fitted with a paddle attachment. Add in 4 pats of canna-butter and pulse for 7 to 10 seconds. Add in the cold butter cubes and pulse two times. Add in the water and pulse three or four times. The dough should look kind of crumbly with big chunks of butter.

2 Turn out the dough onto a floured surface and pull it all together to form a log. Lightly flour the top of the dough and roll it out into a large rectangle. Fold the long sides, one over the other, so you have three layers. Now roll the dough up from end to end. Wrap in plastic wrap and refrigerate for 1 hour.

3 apples

1 teaspoon lemon juice

2 tablespoons raw cane
   sugar

1 teaspoon honey

1 teaspoon rose water

¼ teaspoon ground
   cinnamon

6 tablespoons apricot
   preserves

¼ cup maple syrup

¼ cup Maker's Mark
   bourbon

Confectioners' sugar

PREPARE THE APPLE FILLING

3   Core the apples. Slice each in half and then cut into thin slices. Quickly place the apple slices in a pot and toss with the lemon juice.

4   Add the sugar, honey, rose water, and cinnamon to the pot and fill with water until the apples are submerged by about ½ inch. Bring to a boil and cook for about 2 minutes, until the apples are tender but still slightly crisp. Remove with a slotted spoon and set aside.

CREATE YOUR ROSES

5   Preheat oven to 340°F. Line a muffin tin with butter or paper muffin cups.

6   Unwrap the pastry dough and roll into a large 10-by-12-inch rectangle, ¼ inch thick. Cut the dough into 12 equal strips that are about 1 inch wide and about 10 inches long. Spread a thin layer of apricot preserves along each strip and place 7 to 10 apple slices, slightly overlapping, on top. Carefully roll each strip from end to end and place in the prepared paper muffin cups. Bake for 18 to 20 minutes until lightly golden.

7   In a small bowl, mix together the maple syrup and bourbon. Brush the tops of the apple roses with a little maple-bourbon syrup.

8   Dust with confectioners' sugar and then serve.

Approximate dose per serving is based on infusing 5 grams of cured/dried/decarbed cannabis into 1⅓ sticks of butter.

HEATH BAR CANNA-COOKIE BUTTER BROWNIES

These are my most popular dessert, and there's good reason for it. This is simply a chewy chocolate brownie, with cookie butter, roasted almonds, Heath bar, chocolate . . . and cannabis! Use an ice cream scoop and "mini" baking mold for 24 equally dosed brownies.

Cooking spray (I prefer butter-flavored)

3 sticks grass-fed butter, melted

1 stick creamy canna-butter, melted

3 cups raw cane sugar

1 tablespoon vanilla extract

4 eggs, lightly beaten

1½ cups all-purpose flour

1 cup unsweetened cocoa powder

1 teaspoon salt

1 cup semisweet chocolate chips

½ cup roasted and lightly salted almonds, crushed

1 cup Speculoos cookie butter

1   Preheat oven to 340°F. Lightly grease a 9-by-13-inch brownie pan.

2   Combine the melted butter, melted canna-butter, sugar, and vanilla in a large bowl. Beat in the eggs, one at a time, mixing well after each, until thoroughly blended.

3   Using a flour sifter, sift the flour, cocoa powder, and salt into a separate bowl. (It's important to actually sift these ingredients instead of just tossing them together in a bowl.)

4   Gradually stir the dry mixture into the butter mixture until blended. Add the chocolate chips and almonds. Spread the batter evenly in the prepared baking pan. Bake 35 to 40 minutes, until a toothpick inserted into the center of one or two of the middle brownies comes out clean. Remove, and let the pan cool on a wire rack before releasing the brownies.

5   Cut into 24 equal pieces. Spread a layer of Speculoos cookie butter on top of each brownie and refrigerate uncovered for 30 minutes.

SERVINGS
24

PREP TIME
15
minutes plus 45 minutes for frosting

COOK TIME
35–40
minutes

IDLE TIME
30
minutes

APPROXIMATE THC PER SERVING*

10%:	3.8 mg
15%:	5.7 mg
20%:	7.6 mg

recipe continues

1½ cup melting chocolate—2 colors (1 cup for base color and ½ cup for deco-drizzle)

Paramount Crystals

4 Heath bars or similar, crumbled into pieces

6   In a medium Pyrex bowl, melt the chocolate for your base color with a pinch of Paramount Crystals for 20 seconds in the microwave. Stir well. Microwave again for 10 seconds. Stir briskly until smooth and creamy.

7   Insert a small fork into the side or bottom of a brownie. Dip the brownie in the chocolate, and use a small spatula to ensure that it's evenly coated. Set the coated brownie on parchment paper. Repeat this process with the remaining brownies.

8   Sprinkle Heath Bar crumbles on the brownies while the chocolate is still warm.

9   In a clean bowl, for your decorative color, melt the chocolate with a pinch of Paramount Crystals for 20 seconds in the microwave. Stir well. Microwave again for 10 seconds. Stir briskly until smooth and creamy. Swizzle melted decorative chocolate over brownies, and voilà!

Approximate dose per serving is based on infusing 5 grams of cured/dried/decarbed cannabis into 1⅓ sticks of butter.

WHAT ARE
PARAMOUNT CRYSTALS?

Paramount Crystals are tiny chips of shortening that are the secret to creating a smooth chocolate coating. Your chocolate will be easy to work with and will dry evenly with a nice shiny finish.

CANNA-CARAMEL CORN

I'm a caramel corn fanatic, and the best caramel corn I ever had was at the ArcLight Cinemas in L.A. So it's no surprise that after one night at the movies, I spent a week developing the perfect canna-caramel corn. What you have here is my masterpiece.

12 cups popped popcorn

¾ cup Honey-Whipped Canna-Butter (page 49), plus ¼ cup grass-fed butter

2 cups packed brown sugar

1 teaspoon coarse sea salt

¼ cup light corn syrup

¼ cup dark corn syrup or molasses

1½ teaspoons vanilla extract

1 teaspoon baking soda

1   Preheat oven to 225°F.

2   Pour the popcorn onto a baking sheet lined with parchment paper. Spread evenly.

3   Over medium heat, melt the canna-butter mixture with the brown sugar, sea salt, and light and dark corn syrups. Stir until the sugar dissolves and mixture boils, 5 to 6 minutes. Remove pot from heat and add vanilla. Whisk in the baking soda. The mixture will immediately foam up and double.

4   Drizzle over the popcorn and toss with a rubber or silicone spatula to coat evenly. Bake for 1 hour, using the spatula to toss and mix every 15 minutes.

5   Cool and break apart to serve.

Approximate dose per serving is based on infusing 5 grams of cured/dried/decarbed cannabis into 1⅓ sticks of butter.

SERVINGS

12

PREP TIME

15

minutes

COOK TIME

1

hour

APPROXIMATE THC PER SERVING*

10%: 4 mg

15%: 6 mg

20%: 8 mg

POUNDIN' AMARETTO POUND CAKE

This cake makes for an awesome dessert, and it's great first thing in the morning for breakfast. It also freezes well, in case you want to put some away for a rainy day. My favorite part is the crunchy toasted-almond bottom.

SERVINGS

12

PREP TIME

45

minutes

COOK TIME

1

hour

APPROXIMATE
THC PER
SERVING*

10%: 3.8 mg

15%: 5.7 mg

20%: 7.6 mg

⅓ cup golden raisins

⅓ cup dried cherries

¼ cup Amaretto

3 cups all-purpose flour

½ teaspoon baking soda

¼ teaspoon salt

½ cup Honey-Whipped Canna-Butter (page 49)

2 tablespoons canna-butter

1¾ sticks grass-fed butter, softened

1 (8-ounce) package cream cheese, softened

3 cups raw cane sugar

1 teaspoon almond extract

6 large eggs

½ teaspoon ground cinnamon

½ teaspoon ground nutmeg

1 teaspoon all-purpose flour

1   Preheat oven to 340°F. Grease and flour a round 10-inch Bundt (fluted) pan and set aside.

2   Place raisins and cherries in a small pot with the Amaretto. Bring to a boil, then immediately remove from the heat. Cover and steep for about 20 minutes, until the fruit is plump. Using a slotted spoon, remove the fruit from the Amaretto and set aside. Reserve remaining liquid.

3   In a large bowl, mix together 3 cups flour, baking soda, and salt.

4   In a separate bowl, mix the canna-butters, grass-fed butter, and cream cheese until smooth and creamy. Mix in the sugar, almond extract, and remaining Amaretto liquid from raisins and cherries. Add eggs one at a time, beating well after each.

5   Mix the dry ingredients into the creamed mixture until the batter is smooth. Add the cinnamon and nutmeg.

6   In a separate bowl, combine the 1 teaspoon flour and confectioners' sugar.

1 teaspoon confectioners'
    sugar

Almond slivers, lightly
    toasted

Confectioners' sugar

7   Toss the raisins and cherries in flour mixture to coat. Then fold into the batter.

8   Pour the batter into the Bundt pan. Gently jiggle and tap so that the batter is evenly distributed. Sprinkle almond slivers on top.

9   Bake for 1 hour and 15 minutes, or until a toothpick inserted near the center comes out clean. Remove from oven, and let cool for 15 minutes. Place a plate over the top of the pan and flip. Cool completely.

10   Dust with confectioners' sugar, and serve.

Approximate dose per serving is based on infusing 5 grams of cured/dried/decarbed cannabis into 1⅓ sticks of butter.

Poundin' Amaretto Pound Cake, page 236

STRAWBERRY-BANANA CANNA-CUSTARD NAPOLEON

I love to wow my guests with this beautiful and unexpected infused dessert at the end of dinner parties. It makes a great treat for any celebration or special occasion.

⅓ cup sugar

2 tablespoons cornstarch

¼ teaspoon finely ground sea salt

2 cups whole milk

3 large egg yolks, lightly beaten

3 tablespoons cold creamy canna-butter, cut into small pieces

2 teaspoons vanilla extract

Pastry dough (store-bought)

2 bananas, sliced thin and lightly sugared

1 pint strawberries, sliced thin and lightly sugared

Confectioners' sugar

1   Place a mesh strainer over a mixing bowl and set aside.

2   Combine the sugar, cornstarch, and sea salt in a medium saucepan and whisk until incorporated. While constantly whisking, slowly drizzle in ¼ cup of the milk until smooth. Whisk in the egg yolks and remaining milk.

3   Place the saucepan over medium heat and cook, whisking often, until the pudding begins to thicken and bubble, 5 to 6 minutes. Reduce the heat to medium-low. Stir constantly, scraping the sides and bottom of the pot with a silicone or rubber spatula until pudding thickens enough to hold its form on the spoon (4 to 5 minutes).

4   Remove from the heat and stir in the canna-butter and vanilla extract until the canna-butter is melted and completely incorporated. Pour the pudding through the prepared strainer. Immediately transfer to a medium bowl. Chill in the refrigerator until set, about 2 hours.

SERVINGS

10

PREP TIME

1

hour and 45 minutes

COOK TIME

25–30

minutes

IDLE TIME

2

hours

APPROXIMATE THC PER SERVING*

10%: 3.4 mg

15%: 5.2 mg

20%: 6.9 mg

5   Preheat oven to 340°F.

6   Roll out the pastry dough into a large rectangle, 16 inches by 10 inches by ¼ inch thick. Using a pizza wheel, cut the pastry dough into fifteen 3-inch squares. Bake the pastry squares on a parchment paper–lined baking pan for 18 to 20 minutes, until puffed and golden. Remove and let cool.

7   Slice each puff pastry in half horizontally. Separate out the nicest 10 to use as the tops of the napoleons and another 10 to use as the bottoms. The rest of the pieces will be the middle pastry layer.

8   Lay out the 10 bottom pieces and place ½ teaspoon of custard on each. Layer the banana slices on top of the custard, and add another ½ teaspoon of custard on top of the bananas.

9   Place a "middle" pastry square on top of the bananas and custard. Spread another ½ teaspoon of custard on the "middle" layer, then add the sliced strawberries. Top with ½ teaspoon custard. Place a "top" pastry to cover and sprinkle with confectioners' sugar.

10   Serve to your impressed guests!

*Approximate dose per serving is based on infusing 5 grams of cured/dried/decarbed cannabis into 1⅓ sticks of butter.

SEA SALT CANNA-CARAMEL CORN COOKIES

These are delicious on their own, but for an even more decadent experience, serve them alongside a combination of Tahitian vanilla and coffee ice creams. They are dosed just right so that you can enjoy more than one cookie.

2 cups plus 2 tablespoons all-purpose flour

1 teaspoon baking soda

1 teaspoon baking powder

1 teaspoon salt

1 stick creamy canna-butter, softened

1 stick grass-fed butter, softened

2 large eggs

¾ cup cane sugar

¾ cup packed dark brown sugar

1 teaspoon vanilla extract

1 cup white chocolate chips

1 cup Canna–Caramel Corn (page 235), ½ cup crushed

Sea salt

1   Preheat oven to 340°F.

2   Sift flour, baking soda, baking powder, and salt together in a large bowl.

3   In another bowl, blend the butters together. Add the eggs, sugar, brown sugar, and vanilla extract to butters and blend until creamy and smooth. Slowly add in the flour mixture. Fold in the chocolate chips and ½ cup of crushed Canna–Caramel Corn.

4   Using a small ice cream scoop, drop cookies onto a baking sheet lined with parchment paper. Lightly press a few pieces of the remaining caramel corn onto each cookie, then sprinkle lightly with sea salt. Bake for 10 to 15 minutes or until golden brown.

5   Cool completely and serve.

Approximate dose per serving is based on infusing 5 grams of cured/dried/decarbed cannabis into 1⅓ sticks of butter.

SERVINGS
24
cookies

PREP TIME
30
minutes

COOK TIME
10–15
minutes

APPROXIMATE THC PER SERVING*

10%: 4 mg

15%: 6 mg

20%: 8 mg

STRAWBERRY-LEMON KUSH BARS

When I was growing up, lemon bars were always my treat of choice from the pastry shop (along with a chocolate-chip cookie). Now that I make them myself (and infuse them with cannabis), they are a lot more special. One quick note: I prefer to combine the all-purpose flour with pastry flour for a lighter, flakier crust, but if you prefer a denser crust, you can use just all-purpose flour.

FOR THE TOPPING (MAKE THIS FIRST, IT TAKES 2 HOURS)

½ cup raw cane sugar

½ cup water

½ pint strawberries, rinsed and sliced thin

½ lemon, cut into small triangular wedges

FOR THE CRUST

½ stick creamy canna-butter, plus ½ stick unsalted grass-fed butter, softened

¼ cup cane sugar

⅓ cup all-purpose flour

⅓ cup pastry flour

⅛ teaspoon salt

TO MAKE THE TOPPING

1   Preheat oven to 200°F.

2   In a small saucepan over medium-high heat, bring sugar and ½ cup water to boil, stirring until the sugar has dissolved. Remove from the heat and let cool completely. Dip the strawberries and lemon wedges into the syrup and place on a parchment paper–lined baking sheet. Bake for 2 hours, until the fruit is dried but still colorful. (The lemon wedges should be bright yellow and the strawberries bright red.)

TO MAKE THE CRUST

3   Grease the bottom and sides of an 11-by-7-inch baking pan.

4   In a large bowl, mix together the butters and cane sugar. Add the flour, pastry flour, and salt and blend. Press dough evenly into the buttered pan to fill the bottom. Bake 15 to 18 minutes, until golden.

SERVINGS
12

PREP TIME
2
hours and 20 minutes

COOK TIME
45
minutes

REFRIGERATION TIME
90
minutes

APPROXIMATE THC PER SERVING*

10%: 3.8 mg

15%: 5.7 mg

20%: 7.7 mg

recipe continues

2 eggs

⅔ cup raw cane sugar

3 tablespoons flour

Zest from 1 whole lemon

1 Meyer lemon, juiced

Juice of ½ lime

½ cup buttermilk

5   In a large bowl, whisk the eggs and sugar until smooth. Add the flour, lemon zest, lemon juice, lime juice, and buttermilk. Beat until smooth and no lumps of flour remain. Pour the filling over the baked crust.

6   Bake 20 to 25 minutes until the top looks set and edges begin to turn a light golden brown. Remove from the oven and place in the refrigerator for 90 minutes, until cold and set.

7   Using a sharp knife, cut into 12 pieces, top with candied strawberry and lemon slices, and serve.

*Approximate dose per serving is based on infusing 5 grams of cured/dried/decarbed cannabis into 1⅓ sticks of butter.

THE DOUBLE-WHAMMY ICE CREAM SANDWICH

My friends call this the king of ice cream sandwiches. The cookies are an elevated twist on the original Toll House cookie recipe, featuring Blazed Pecans and canna-butter, and the sandwich is an ode to my favorite ice cream treat to this day, the famed Chipwich. Each cookie contains cannabis, so dose accordingly.

SERVINGS
12

PREP TIME
30
minutes

COOK TIME
10–15
minutes

APPROXIMATE
THC PER
SERVING*

10%: 8.2 mg

15%: 12.4 mg

20%: 16.4 mg

2¼ cups all-purpose flour

1 teaspoon baking soda

1 teaspoon salt

1 stick creamy canna-butter, softened

1 stick grass-fed butter, softened

2 large eggs

¾ cup cane sugar

¾ cup packed dark brown sugar

1 teaspoon vanilla extract

1 cup semisweet chocolate chips

1 cup Blazed Pecans (page 78)

Your favorite ice cream

1   Preheat oven to 340°F.

2   Sift flour, baking soda, and salt together in a large bowl.

3   In a separate bowl, blend the canna-butter and the grass-fed butter together. Add the eggs, sugar, brown sugar, and vanilla extract to butters and blend until creamy and smooth. Slowly add the flour mixture. Fold in the chocolate chips and Blazed Pecans.

4   Using a small ice cream scoop, drop 24 cookies onto baking sheet lined with parchment paper. Bake for 11 to 15 minutes, or until golden brown (shorten the time for chewy cookies; lengthen the time for crispy cookies). Let them cool completely and then freeze for 30 minutes.

5   To complete the sandwiches, press one scoop of ice cream between 2 cookies. Refreeze for 1 hour and serve.

*Approximate dose per serving is based on infusing 5 grams of cured/dried/decarbed cannabis into 1⅓ sticks of butter.

MAPLE CREAM CANNA-PUFFS PARTY TOWER

This is the ultimate party cake and a beautiful dessert centerpiece. Each cream puff is lightly medicated, so you and your guests can enjoy more than just one or two. Just make sure you pay attention to the percentage of THC in the butter you use, and let your guests know approximately how many milligrams of THC there are in each puff so they don't go overboard.

FOR THE MAPLE CANNA-CUSTARD

4 tablespoons maple syrup

2 tablespoons cornstarch

¼ teaspoon finely ground sea salt

2 cups whole milk

3 large egg yolks, lightly beaten

3 tablespoons cold creamy canna-butter, cut into small pieces

2 teaspoons vanilla extract

TO PREPARE THE CUSTARD

1   Place a mesh strainer over a mixing bowl and set aside.

2   Combine the maple syrup, cornstarch, and sea salt in a medium saucepan and whisk until incorporated. While constantly whisking, slowly drizzle in ¼ cup of the milk until smooth. Whisk in the egg yolks and remaining milk.

3   Place the saucepan over medium heat and cook, whisking often, until the pudding begins to thicken and bubble, 5 to 6 minutes. Reduce the heat to medium-low. Stir constantly, scraping the sides and bottom of the pot with a silicone or rubber spatula until pudding thickens enough to hold its form on the spoon (4 to 5 minutes).

4   Remove from the heat and stir in the canna-butter and vanilla extract until the canna-butter is melted and completely incorporated. Pour the pudding through the prepared strainer and immediately transfer to a medium bowl. Chill in the refrigerator until set, about 2 hours.

recipe continues

FOR THE CANNA-PUFFS

3 eggs, plus 1 egg for egg wash

1 cup water

1 stick unsalted grass-fed butter

½ teaspoon salt

1½ teaspoons raw cane sugar

1 cup all-purpose flour

2 cups canna-custard

FOR CARAMEL "GLUE"

1 cup heavy cream

1 tablespoon creamy canna-butter, plus 2 tablespoons unsalted grass-fed butter

¼ teaspoon salt

1½ cups white granulated sugar

¼ cup corn syrup

¼ cup water

½ teaspoon vanilla extract

TO PREPARE THE CANNA-PUFFS

5   Preheat oven to 425°F.

6   Beat 1 egg in a small bowl and set aside as your egg wash.

7   In a large saucepan, bring the water, butter, salt, and raw cane sugar to a rolling boil over medium-high heat. Immediately remove from heat and add all the flour at once. Stir vigorously until all the flour is incorporated, about 1 minute.

8   Return the saucepan to the heat and cook for less than a minute to dry the mixture out a bit. Then fully beat the 3 eggs, one at a time, into the flour mixture. Mix until the dough is smooth and glossy and the eggs are completely incorporated.

9   Using an ice cream scoop with a release lever, drop 30 dough balls onto a parchment paper–lined baking pan. Brush the top of each dough ball with the egg wash.

10   Bake for 15 minutes at 425°F, then reduce heat to 375°F and continue baking for 18 to 20 minutes, until the balls are puffed and golden. Do not open the oven while they are baking. Remove and let cool.

TO FILL THE PUFFS

11   Remove the canna-custard from the refrigerator and scrape off the skin (this is yours to enjoy while you make the cream puffs). Fit a pastry bag with a pastry tip. Insert the tip into the puffs, one at a time, and squeeze about 1 tablespoon of custard into each puff.

12   Refrigerate the filled puffs, covered lightly with plastic wrap so they don't get soggy.

TO PREPARE THE CANNA-CARAMEL "GLUE"

13   Over medium heat, warm the cream, canna-butter mixture, and salt in a 2-quart saucepan until the butter melts. Remove from the heat.

14   In a large saucepan, combine the sugar, corn syrup, and water. Stir to create a thick grainy paste. Wipe down the insides of the pan with a damp pastry brush or rubber spatula so there are no sugar crystals above the surface of the mixture. Cook over medium to medium-high heat. Do not stir. Let the sugar syrup come to a boil. Boil untouched until the sugar begins to turn light brown and to smell like caramel.

1½ cups melting chocolate (it's fun to choose a color that matches the occasion)

Paramount Crystals

¼ cup hazelnuts, toasted and lightly crushed

15 Turn off the heat and whisk in the warm cream mixture. Return the pan to medium to medium-high heat. Let the caramel come to a boil again without stirring. When the caramel turns a reddish-brown or caramel color, remove it from the heat. Immediately whisk in the vanilla.

16 Let the mixture sit for 30 to 45 minutes to cool enough so you can put it into a pastry bag and work with the bag.

TO CREATE THE TOWER

17 Fit a pastry bag with a small or small/medium tip and fill the bag with the caramel.

18 Arrange 7 puffs in a circle on a platter. Pipe a stripe of caramel on the seams connecting each puff. Place 6 puffs on the next layer, centering each puff on the caramel seam below. Now pipe a stripe of caramel on the seams connecting each puff on this layer. Repeat this process until you have 7 levels, with one puff on the top.

19 Save the remaining 2 canna-puffs for you and a friend.

TO DECORATE THE TOWER

20 In a medium Pyrex bowl, melt the chocolate with a large pinch of Paramount Crystals for 20 seconds in the microwave. Stir well. Microwave again for 10 seconds. Stir briskly until smooth and creamy and fluid.

21 Slowly pour a light stream of melted chocolate from the top of the tower so it drips down the sides. Garnish with crushed hazelnuts, and then present your masterpiece!

Approximate dose per serving is based on infusing 5 grams of cured/dried/decarbed cannabis into 1⅓ sticks of butter.

SEA-SALTED CANNA-BUTTER PRETZELS WITH CARAMEL SAUCE

Inspired by a trip to Auntie Anne's pretzels in New York City, this was my first non-cookie/non-brownie cannabis-infused recipe. Soft, chewy, and deliciously medicated, they are now a staple at many of my 420 dinner parties.

SERVINGS
12

PREP TIME
25
minutes

COOK TIME
8
minutes

IDLE TIME
1
hour to 1 hour and
30 minutes

APPROXIMATE
THC PER
SERVING*
10%: 7.7 mg
15%: 11.5 mg
20%: 15.4 mg

FOR THE PRETZELS

2 tablespoons packed light brown sugar

2 tablespoons granulated sugar

1 cup milk

1 cup water

1½ tablespoons active dry yeast (2 packets)

4 tablespoons grass-fed butter, softened

4½ cups all-purpose flour

2 teaspoons fine sea salt

¼ cup baking soda

1 cup warm water

1 stick creamy canna-butter, melted

Kosher salt

TO PREPARE THE PRETZELS

1   In a small bowl, mix the sugars and set aside.

2   In a small saucepan, warm the milk and water over medium-low heat until the temperature reaches 110°F, 1½ to 2 minutes. Pour the warm milk-and-water mixture into a large bowl and whisk in the yeast until it has dissolved. Let rest for 5 to 7 minutes until it foams.

3   Add the sugars, grass-fed butter, 1 cup flour, and 2 teaspoons fine sea salt to the milk mixture. Stir until blended. Slowly add the remaining 3½ cups flour and knead until elastic. The dough should pull away from the sides of the bowl.

4   Cover the bowl with plastic wrap and allow the dough to rise in a warm place until doubled in size, 60 to 90 minutes. Don't go by time—go by results.

5   Preheat oven to 450°F.

½ cup heavy cream

½ cup raw cane sugar

½ cup light brown sugar

¼ cup water

1 tablespoon light corn
syrup

2 tablespoons unsalted
grass-fed butter,
softened

1 teaspoon pure vanilla
extract

6   Punch down the dough and divide it into 12 equal pieces. Cover dough portions loosely with plastic wrap while you work, to prevent a dry crust from forming on the outside.

7   Roll each piece out into a long, thin rope. The dough will rise, so thin is the key here. Now tie each rope into a large loose knot (so it looks like a pretzel).

8   In a shallow bowl, whisk together the baking soda and warm water.

9   Fully immerse each pretzel in baking soda bath for a few seconds, then place on a baking pan lined with parchment paper. Bake the pretzels in a preheated oven for 7 to 9 minutes, until golden brown (8 minutes seems to be the magic number for my oven). Remove from the oven and brush the tops and bottoms of pretzels with the melted canna-butter. Sprinkle them with kosher salt.

TO PREPARE THE CARAMEL SAUCE

10   In a small pot, heat the cream until scalding hot (just below a boil) and set aside.

11   In a large pot, combine the sugars, water, and corn syrup and bring to a boil over medium-high heat. Stir until the sugars are dissolved and continue cooking, without stirring, until the mixture reaches 380°F.

12   Remove from the heat and slowly add the cream. The mixture will foam, so be careful. Slowly add in the butter and vanilla, and continue to mix until smooth.

13   Bring the mixture back to a boil and boil for 5 minutes, until the caramel forms silky ribbons when drizzled over itself.

14   Remove from heat and let cool for 10 minutes.

15   Serve warm with pretzels.

Approximate dose per serving is based on infusing 5 grams of cured/dried/decarbed cannabis into 1⅓ sticks of butter.

PUMPKIN SPICE SNACK CAKE

SERVINGS

12

PREP TIME

30

minutes

COOK TIME

45–50

minutes

APPROXIMATE
THC PER
SERVING*

10%: 5 mg

15%: 7.6 mg

20%: 10 mg

Chef J. P. Reyes and I invite you to enjoy a slice (or two) of fall goodness with this tasty, vegan pumpkin spice cake. If you prefer a more buttery cake, just use ¼ cup canna-butter instead of the canna–coconut oil.

3 cups all-purpose flour

1 teaspoon baking soda

½ teaspoon salt

1 teaspoon freshly grated nutmeg

2 teaspoons ground cinnamon

½ teaspoon ground ginger

½ teaspoon ground cloves

½ teaspoon ground allspice

½ teaspoon ground cardamom

¼ cup grass-fed butter, melted

2 tablespoons extra-virgin canna–coconut oil, plus 2 tablespoons extra-virgin coconut oil

3 large eggs

2 cups raw cane sugar

1 teaspoon vanilla extract

1 (15-ounce) can pumpkin puree

1   Preheat oven to 325°F. Grease and flour a 9-by-5-inch loaf pan and set aside.

2   In a large bowl, mix the flour, baking soda, and salt. Mix in the nutmeg, cinnamon, ginger, cloves, allspice, and cardamom and stir to distribute the spices throughout the flour mixture.

3   In a separate bowl, mix the grass-fed butter, canna–coconut oil mixture, eggs, sugar, vanilla, and pumpkin puree until smooth.

4   Add the dry ingredients to the wet ingredients and mix until smooth. Pour into the prepared pan and bake for 75 to 90 minutes, until a toothpick inserted into the center comes out clean.

5   Let cool partially for 20 minutes and serve warm.

*Approximate dose per serving is based on infusing 5 grams of cured/dried/decarbed cannabis into 5 ounces of oil.

Mediterranean Chicken, Roasted Canna-Spiked Eggplant & Couscous, page 277

CHAPTER NO.10

Entertaining &
Gourmet

POACHED SALMON, SAUTÉED ZUCCHINI & LEEK SPAGHETTI, BEURRE BLANC & PARSLEYED POTATOES

SERVINGS
6

PREP TIME
45
minutes

COOK TIME
1
hour and 30
minutes

APPROXIMATE
THC PER
SERVING*

10%: 5.1 mg

15%: 7.6 mg

20%: 10.2 mg

This elegant and incredibly delicious 420 salmon meal results from a collaboration between Chef Tadashi Miwa and me. Tadashi and I met when he was working the line at One Market in San Francisco. I always thought poaching salmon would be difficult, but Tadashi showed me that it's easier than making pie in a store-bought pie shell—and it takes only minutes! Want a neat trick for the zucchini-and-leek spaghetti? Get a $15 hand spiralizer! This is my new favorite kitchen gadget and it "spaghettis" a whole zucchini in only 30 seconds.

FOR THE SALMON

6 salmon fillets (about 6 ounces each)

Fine sea salt

White pepper

FOR THE COURT BOUILLON (POACHING LIQUID)

4 medium yellow onions, roughly chopped

8 carrots, chopped (about 1 inch thick)

8 celery stalks, chopped (about 1 inch thick)

⅔ cup white wine vinegar

5 quarts water

1 herb sachet of 3 sprigs thyme, 5 parsley stems, 1 bay leaf, 1 teaspoon cracked peppercorns

1   Season both sides of salmon with salt and white pepper to taste.

PREPARE THE COURT BOUILLON

2   In a large pot, place all of the ingredients (except the sachet) in the water and bring to a boil. Reduce the heat to low and allow to simmer. Add the sachet and allow bouillon to simmer for 45 minutes to 1 hour. You should be able to taste the acid and the aromatics. Strain and keep hot over very low heat.

recipe continues

12 baby red potatoes,
washed and cut in
quarters

Salt

2 tablespoons grass-fed
butter

¼ cup parsley, minced

FOR THE BEURRE
BLANC

2 teaspoons shallot,
minced

½ teaspoon black
peppercorns

½ cup dry white wine

1 tablespoon lemon juice

1½ tablespoons cider or
white wine vinegar

¼ cup heavy cream

1¾ sticks grass-fed butter,
cubed (about 1 inch)
and chilled

2 tablespoons creamy
canna-butter, chilled

Salt

Ground white pepper

BOIL THE POTATOES

3   In a separate large pot, place the baby red potatoes, quartered, and
cover with water. Season with salt and allow to simmer over medium heat
until cooked, 15 to 18 minutes. Do not boil—if you do, the potatoes will
start to fall apart as they cook.

4   Remove the potatoes and soak in an ice bath to stop the cooking
process, then set aside.

PREPARE THE BEURRE BLANC

5   Combine the shallot, peppercorns, wine, lemon juice, and vinegar in a
saucepan. Cook over medium-high heat until the liquid has evaporated to
nearly dry. Add the heavy cream and reduce by half over medium heat.

6   Lower the heat and allow the cream to barely simmer. Add the cubed/
chilled butter and canna-butter a few pieces at a time, whisking constantly
to incorporate thoroughly. When all of the butter is incorporated, the
sauce will be slightly thickened.

7   Taste and season with salt and white pepper. Set aside and hold in a
warm space.

PREPARE THE POACHED SALMON

8   Bring the court bouillon to a bare simmer.

9   Submerge the seasoned salmon fillets fully (about 2 inches deep from
the surface) and poach for 7 to 10 minutes. After 7 minutes, check the
internal temperature of the salmon (it must be at least 125° but no more
than 135°F). Set aside and cover to keep warm.

2 teaspoons grass-fed
butter

2 teaspoons creamy
canna-butter

1½ cups zucchini, cut into
a long julienne (⅛ by ⅛
inch thick)

1½ cups leeks, white part
only, cut into a long
julienne and blanched

Salt

Ground black pepper

1 tablespoon chives,
minced

PREPARE THE PARSLEYED POTATOES

10 In a sauté pan, heat the grass-fed butter over medium-high heat. Toss
in the prepared potatoes and sauté until there is some browning on the
surface of the potatoes. Remove from the heat, season with salt, and toss in
a generous amount of parsley.

PREPARE THE ZUCCHINI—AND—LEEK SPAGHETTI

11 In a separate sauté pan, heat the grass-fed butter over medium heat.
When melted, add in canna-butter and mix well.

12 Immediately add the zucchini and leeks, tossing frequently until
heated through (2 to 3 minutes). Season with salt and black pepper.
Remove from the heat and toss in the chopped chives.

TO PLATE

13 Place a fair amount of the sautéed zucchini-and-leek spaghetti in the
center of the plate. Position a poached salmon fillet on top of the bed of
noodles. Place a serving of the parsleyed potatoes on the side. Ladle about
2 tablespoons of the beurre blanc sauce on top of the salmon, and serve.

*Approximate dose per serving is based on infusing 5 grams of cured/dried/decarbed cannabis
into 1⅓ sticks of butter.*

BEEF TARTARE, CROSTINI, EGG YOLK & ARUGULA SALAD

This perfectly dosed appetizer is another fun collaboration with Chef Tadashi. The flavor of the capers and herbs mixed with the subtle flavor of the cannabis complements the fresh taste of the beef. Placed on a bed of arugula and topped with a creamy egg yolk, this dish is wonderfully tasty and makes for a beautiful presentation.

6 eggs

¾ cup olive oil

2 tablespoons capers

1 cup crème fraîche

2 tablespoons horseradish root, grated

4 teaspoons lemon juice

Salt and freshly ground black pepper

2 pounds New York strip or rib eye steak (fat cap, gristle, and sinews removed), diced small

8 tablespoons shallots, finely diced (about 2 large shallots)

4 tablespoons tarragon, minced

3 tablespoons chives, minced

4 tablespoons chervil, minced (optional)

7 lemons (zest only)

1   Preheat a grill or broiler.

2   In a pot, simmer water on very low heat (about 140°F). Place the eggs in the pot, making sure that the water covers the eggs by at least ½ inch. Cook for 4 minutes.

3   Heat a large skillet over high heat for about 2 minutes. Add ¼ cup of olive oil and the capers and fry until crispy, about 5 minutes. (*Note:* When capers are fried, they bloom like a flower, which will provide visual appeal to the dish.) Remove the capers from the oil and spread on a paper towel. Set aside at room temperature. Reserve the oil to make the crostini.

4   In a medium bowl, whisk the crème fraîche until slightly foamy and aerated. Add the grated horseradish root and lemon juice, then season to taste with salt and pepper. Mix thoroughly. Taste and adjust the flavors and seasoning as necessary.

recipe continues

SERVINGS
6

PREP TIME
1
hour

COOK TIME
1
hour

APPROXIMATE THC PER SERVING*

10%: 5 mg

15%: 7.6 mg

20%: 10 mg

¼ cup extra-virgin olive oil

1 tablespoon extra-virgin canna–olive oil, plus 3 tablespoons extra-virgin olive oil

3 tablespoons capers, minced

3 tablespoons caper juice

24 slices French bread, cut on the bias, ¼ inch thick

6 handfuls baby arugula

5   Transfer the mixture into a piping bag and set aside in the fridge.

6   In a separate bowl, toss diced steak, shallots, tarragon, chives, chervil, half of the lemon zest, ¼ cup extra-virgin olive oil, canna–olive oil mixture, minced capers, and caper juice. Season with salt and pepper. Set aside in the fridge.

7   Brush the sliced bread with the olive oil you used to fry the capers, and season lightly with salt (the capers already have a lot of salty flavor). Toast on the preheated grill or under the broiler until golden brown and crispy.

8   In another bowl, toss the arugula with the remaining extra-virgin olive oil, add the remaining lemon zest, and season with salt and pepper. Taste and adjust seasoning as necessary.

9   To plate, divide the tartare into 6 portions, and place each portion on the plate in a neat pile (use a mold, if desired). Crack the soft-boiled egg atop the tartare. Pipe dollops of crème fraîche around or on top of one side of the tartare (use your imagination here). Place crispy capers atop each dollop of crème fraîche, or randomly sprinkle them on the plate. Place the arugula salad on one side with the crostini, and serve.

Approximate dose per serving is based on infusing 5 grams of cured/dried/decarbed cannabis into 5 ounces of oil.

SHAPOT DINNER

This is the meal that makes my mom the proudest. It's the real-deal "Shabbat meal," complete with Gefilte Fish, Potzo Ball Soup, and Canna-Challah. It pairs beautifully with the Infused BBQ Pulled Brisket (page 176) to create the complete experience. Time for an uplifting Shabbat dinner!

FULL MEAL
(not including the Infused BBQ Pulled Brisket)*

SERVINGS
6

PREP TIME
2
hours and 30 minutes

COOK TIME
4
hours

APPROXIMATE THC PER SERVING

10%: 7.1 mg

15%: 10.7 mg

20%: 14.2 mg

Infused Gefilte Fish

SERVINGS
6

APPROXIMATE
THC PER
SERVING*

10%: 1.67 mg

15%: 2.5 mg

20%: 3.3 mg

½ cup matzo meal

4 cups fish or vegetable stock

4 carrots

1 large onion, halved and sliced

2 stalks celery, sliced

2 teaspoons honey

3 tablespoons olive oil

1 medium onion, minced

2 garlic cloves, minced

1 teaspoon light canna-olive oil

2 pounds whitefish, carp, or salmon

3 eggs, separated

1 tablespoon raw cane sugar

1 teaspoon parsley, chopped

2 to 3 teaspoons salt

½ teaspoon ground white pepper

1   Place the matzo meal in a small bowl. Cover with 1 cup of stock and let soak.

2   Preheat oven to 340°F.

3   In a small saucepan, heat the remaining stock, carrots, sliced onion, celery, and honey until it boils. Immediately remove from heat and pour into a large baking dish. Set aside.

4   Preheat a small skillet and heat the regular olive oil. Over medium heat, sauté the minced onion until translucent, 3 to 4 minutes. Do not brown. Add garlic and canna-oil and sauté for 1 more minute. Remove from heat and let cool.

5   In a food processor, chop the fish until fine. Add the wet matzo meal, sautéed onion, 3 egg yolks, sugar, chopped parsley, 2 teaspoons salt, and white pepper. Pulse until well combined.

6   In a clean medium bowl, whisk the egg whites until firm. Gently fold the egg whites into the fish mixture. Add salt and pepper to taste.

7   Divide the fish mixture into 12 equal parts and shape each into a 5-inch log. Set the logs into the stock-filled baking dish. Cover with aluminum foil and bake for 30 to 35 minutes.

8   Let cool with stock, refrigerate, and serve when ready.

Approximate dose per serving is based on infusing 5 grams of cured/dried/decarbed cannabis into 5 ounces of oil.

Chocolate-Filled Canna-Challah

FOR THE CHALLAH

2 cups high-gluten flour, plus more as needed

2 cups whole-wheat flour

1 cup warm water (about 110°F)

1 package dry yeast

1 teaspoon sugar

1 tablespoon extra-virgin canna–coconut oil, plus 3 tablespoons extra-virgin coconut oil

2 eggs, beaten

¼ cup honey

1½ teaspoons salt

1 cup bittersweet chocolate chips (6 ounces)

FOR THE TOPPING

1 egg for egg wash

1 teaspoon water for egg wash

2 tablespoons sugar

¼ teaspoon cinnamon

1   Sift together the high-gluten flour and whole-wheat flour. Set aside.

2   In a large mixing bowl, stir together the warm water, yeast, and sugar. Let stand for about 5 minutes, until it starts to look foamy. Whisk in the canna–coconut oil mixture, 2 eggs, honey, and salt and mix until well combined. Add the flour mixture and stir until everything is combined and dough is starting to form. Be aware that the dough might be sticky at this point.

3   Turn the dough out onto a well-floured surface and knead for about 10 minutes, until the dough is no longer sticky and it bounces back when you indent it with your finger. Place in a well-greased mixing bowl, cover with plastic wrap or a plate, and let it rise for about 1 hour at room temperature, until doubled in size. Then place the dough in the refrigerator to develop flavor and rise overnight.

4   When you're ready to bake, grease two 8-inch cake pans.

5   Cut the dough into two proportional pieces and cover the second with a kitchen towel. Working with the first piece of dough, cut it into 8 equal pieces. For each of these small pieces, place 2 teaspoons of chocolate chips in the center and pinch the dough around the chocolate. Roll it into a ball, keeping a pocket of chocolate chips inside.

recipe continues

6   Place these 8 balls in one of your greased tins, with one in the center and the other balls arranged evenly around it.

7   Repeat this process with the second ball of dough and arrange the balls in the second greased tin. Cover both tins and let the dough rise for 60 to 90 minutes. The balls of dough should rise and join together and become light and airy. If they aren't doubled in size after 1 hour, let them rise an additional 30 minutes and check again.

8   Meanwhile, preheat oven to 375°F.

TO PREPARE THE TOPPING

9   Beat the remaining egg with 1 teaspoon water, and brush over the challah. Mix the sugar and cinnamon together and sprinkle evenly over the challah. Bake for 30 to 40 minutes, checking after the first 20 minutes. If the challah is browning too quickly, lightly cover it with foil. Remove from the oven, and let cool on a wire rack.

*Approximate dose per serving is based on infusing 5 grams of cured/dried/decarbed cannabis into 5 ounces of oil.

Chicken Soup

POTZO
BALLS

SERVINGS
6
potzo balls

APPROXIMATE
THC PER
SERVING*

10%: 2.6 mg

15%: 3.8 mg

20%: 5.2 mg

FOR THE CHICKEN
SOUP

1 whole chicken, 3 to 4
pounds

1 celery root

4 quarts water

4 large carrots, halved

4 stalks celery, halved
(including leaves)

2 parsnips, halved

1 turnip, quartered

1 Spanish onion, skin on,
rinsed and sliced in two
halves

5 to 6 sprigs fresh parsley

5 to 6 sprigs fresh dill

2 sprigs thyme

2 teaspoons black
peppercorns

3 to 5 whole cloves

½ teaspoon turmeric

4 or 5 strings of saffron

2 bay leaves

4 tablespoons kosher salt

⅓ cup carrots, peeled and
sliced

⅓ cup celery, sliced

¼ cup fresh dill, chopped

¼ cup fresh parsley,
chopped

1   Place the chicken and celery root in a very large pot with 4 quarts of water and boil for 15 minutes. Place the halved carrots and celery (including leaves), parsnips, turnip, Spanish onion halves, and sprigs of parsley, dill, and thyme in a large piece of cheesecloth or a soup sock. Shut and secure with a piece of twine.

2   Lower the heat on the pot to simmer and, using a ladle, remove the foam, etc., that rises to the top. Place vegetable sachet in the pot and cover with more water, if necessary. Add peppercorns, cloves, turmeric, saffron, bay leaves, and kosher salt. Bring to a boil, then cover and lower heat to simmer. Simmer for 90 minutes.

3   While soup is cooking, make the potzo balls.

recipe continues

FOR THE POTZO BALLS

3 eggs

2 teaspoons canna-olive
    oil, plus 2 tablespoons
    light olive oil

1 teaspoon onion, minced
    fine

Splash of club soda

¾ cup matzo meal

1 teaspoon baking powder

Salt

Coarsely ground pepper

TO MAKE THE POTZO BALLS

4   In a medium bowl, whisk eggs with canna-olive oil mixture. Add minced onion. Add club soda and stir.

5   In a separate bowl, combine the matzo meal and baking powder, then fold into the egg mixture. Add salt and pepper to taste. Cover with plastic wrap and refrigerate for 30 minutes.

TO MAKE POTZO BALL SOUP

6   Remove the soup from heat and let cool for 30 minutes. Remove everything from the pot but the liquid, and discard the vegetable sachet and celery root.

7   Cut, dice, or shred chicken and set aside.

8   Place the soup back on stove and bring to a boil. Using an ice cream scoop, drop 6 potzo balls into the boiling soup liquid. Boil for 10 minutes until balls set.

9   Add back the chicken, then add the sliced carrots, celery, chopped dill, and parsley. Continue to cook for 20 minutes and then serve.

Approximate dose per serving is based on infusing 5 grams of cured/dried/decarbed cannabis into 5 ounces of oil.

NOTE

I suggest that you "cut" the cannabis oil in all the infused dishes to achieve a maximum of 15–20 milligrams THC per person total for the meal.

TO COMPLETE THE MEAL

Serve with Infused BBQ Pulled Brisket (page 176), Zucchini Canna-Kugel (page 173), or Five-Pepper Blazed POTatoes (page 122). Top it off with Canna-Apple Roses (page 230) or Pumpkin Spice Snack Cake (page 254) for dessert.

GRILLED STEAK WITH COMPOUND CANNA-BUTTER, JUS, GRILLED SEASONAL VEGETABLES & POTATO PUREE

Another collaboration with Chef Tadashi, this is the ultimate bistro steak dinner. What can be better than compound butter melting over a sizzling steak? Compound canna-butter—enjoy!

FULL MEAL

SERVINGS
6

PREP TIME
1
hour

COOK TIME
1
hour and 30 minutes

APPROXIMATE THC PER SERVING*

10%: 7.3 mg

15%: 11 mg

20%: 14.6 mg

JUS LIÉ

1 pound chicken bones, including trimmings, like wings and some meat

4 tablespoons light olive oil

¼ cup carrots, medium dice (½ inch by ½ inch)

¼ cup celery, medium dice

½ cup yellow onion, medium dice

2 tablespoons tomato paste

½ cup dry red wine

4 cups chicken stock

1 sachet of 5 sprigs thyme, 6 parsley stems, 1 bay leaf, 1 teaspoon cracked peppercorns

2 tablespoons cornstarch mixed into 1 cup of water (slurry)

Salt

Ground black pepper

PREPARE THE JUS LIÉ

1   In a large pot, brown the chicken bones and the trimmings in the oil over medium-high heat. Remove the browned chicken bones and trimmings and set aside.

2   In the same pan, add the carrot, celery, and onion (in that order, cooking them at least 1 minute apart) until they brown. Pour off the excess oil, then add the tomato paste and cook, stirring frequently (adjust to medium heat), until brick-brown and giving off a sweet aroma (15 to 20 minutes).

3   Add the red wine to deglaze the pan and reduce the wine slightly. Add the chicken stock and stir to release the drippings from the bottom of the pan, then add back the browned chicken bones and trimmings.

4   Reduce heat to medium-low or low, then add the herb sachet. Simmer and start reducing the *jus lié* until desired concentration of flavor is achieved (about 30 minutes). While reducing the *jus lié*, use a ladle to continuously degrease and remove the impurities at the surface.

FOR THE COMPOUND CANNA-BUTTER

3¾ sticks unsalted grass-fed butter

2 tablespoons creamy canna-butter, softened at room temperature

1 tablespoon thyme, minced

1 tablespoon chives, minced

1 tablespoon parsley, minced

Salt

FOR THE POTATO PUREE

6 medium russet potatoes

1 cup crème fraîche

1¾ sticks grass-fed butter

1 tablespoon creamy canna-butter plus 1 tablespoon salted grass-fed butter

1 cup chives, minced

Salt

Pepper

5   Add the cornstarch slurry to thicken the sauce enough to coat the back of a spoon. Adjust seasoning with salt and pepper.

6   Strain through a chinois or a fine-mesh strainer; set aside the sauce and keep it in a hot place. Any extra sauce can be kept in the fridge for a couple of weeks for future use.

PREPARE THE COMPOUND CANNA-BUTTER

7   In a bowl, mix together the softened butter, canna-butter, minced thyme, chives, and parsley. Season well with salt. Place the butter mixture in a plastic wrap and roll into a log, making sure that the roll is tight and no air pockets are present. If there are air pockets, poke the air pockets with a toothpick to release the air, then retighten the roll. Refrigerate to solidify.

PREPARE THE POTATO PUREE

8   Preheat oven to 340°F, and bake the potatoes for 1 hour.

9   While still hot, but cool enough to work with, cut the potatoes lengthwise and scoop out the insides with a spoon into a mixing bowl. Mash the potatoes and add the crème fraîche, butter, canna-butter, and minced chives (fold gently with a spatula, being careful not to overmash). Season with salt and pepper. Set aside and keep hot.

COMPOUND CANNA-BUTTER

APPROXIMATE THC PER SERVING*

10%: 3.8 mg

15%: 5.7 mg

20%: 7.6 mg

BAKED POTATOES

APPROXIMATE THC PER SERVING*

10%: 1.9 mg

15%: 2.8 mg

20%: 3.8 mg

---

*Approximate dose per serving is based on infusing 5 grams of cured/dried/decarbed cannabis into 1⅓ sticks of butter

recipe continues

FOR THE CANDIED BABY CARROTS

1 pound baby carrots, peeled and ends trimmed

1 teaspoon canna-olive oil, plus 1 tablespoon olive oil

2 teaspoons brown sugar

Pinch of salt

Pinch of cinnamon

FOR THE STEAK

Vegetable oil for seasoning grill

6 (8-ounce) grass-fed rib eye steaks (¾ inch to 1 inch thick)

Salt

Ground black pepper

PREPARE THE BABY CARROTS

10   Keep the oven at 340°F.

11   Drizzle the baby carrots with the canna-olive oil mixture, brown sugar, a pinch of salt, and a pinch of cinnamon. Coat evenly, then spread out on a baking sheet.

12   Roast the baby carrots (during the last 15 to 20 minutes of the potatoes' baking) until some surface caramelization develops. Check for doneness, and cook longer if necessary. Set aside and keep in a hot place.

PREPARE THE GRILL

13   Make sure grill is clean, and preheat it to medium-high. Season the grill by wiping it with cloth dampened with vegetable oil as you allow it to heat up.

14   Season the steaks thoroughly with salt and pepper. Place the steaks on the grill for about 2 minutes, then rotate each steak 90° in the same spot on the grill for another 2 minutes. Repeat the same process on the other side of the steak. Finish cooking the steak either on the grill or in the oven (internal temperature must be at least 125°F for nice medium-rare steak).

TO PLATE

15   Spoon the desired amount of potato puree onto the plate at about the three o'clock position. Place the steak at about six o'clock, leaning it a little on the potatoes. Ladle in the sauce, pouring over only one part of the steak. Place a slice of compound butter atop the steak. Position the roasted baby carrots at about ten o'clock, and serve immediately.

CANDIED BABY CARROTS

APPROXIMATE THC PER SERVING*

10%: 1.6 mg

15%: 2.5 mg

20%: 3.2 mg

*Approximate dose per serving is based on infusing 5 grams of cured/dried/decarbed cannabis into 1⅓ sticks of butter.

MEDITERRANEAN CHICKEN, ROASTED CANNA-SPIKED EGGPLANT & COUSCOUS

Several years ago while visiting the Isle of Capri, I met a man who made me a delicious dish of chicken with spiced eggplant. He also taught me a few culinary tricks, like scoring, salting, and adding red pepper flakes to the eggplant before roasting. As soon as I got back, I re-created the recipe, added a few ingredients of my own (including a very special one), and voilà! The dish is simple, exotic, comforting, and lighter on the cannabis. And because the cannabis is infused into the eggplant only, you can serve this to a mixed crowd, in which some want cannabis and others don't. Simply leave off the eggplant for the people who want to dine without cannabis.

SERVINGS

4

PREP TIME

30

minutes

COOK TIME

40

minutes

APPROXIMATE THC PER SERVING*

10%: 2.5 mg

15%: 3.8 mg

20%: 5 mg

FOR THE EGGPLANT

1 large eggplant, cut into 1-inch-thick steaks

½ cup olive oil

½ teaspoon fine sea salt

½ teaspoon red pepper flakes, plus more to taste

1 teaspoon canna-olive oil, plus 1 tablespoon extra-virgin olive oil

1 teaspoon fennel seeds

Juice of 1 lemon

ROAST THE EGGPLANT

1   Preheat oven to 400°F.

2   Slice a "crosshatch" diamond pattern into each side of the eggplant steaks.

3   Brush both sides of each steak with olive oil and sprinkle with fine sea salt and red pepper flakes. Place the eggplant steaks on a cookie sheet lined with parchment paper and roast for 20 minutes on each side. Remove the skin, and dice the eggplant flesh into 1-inch cubes.

4   Place the eggplant in a large bowl, and drizzle with canna-olive oil mixture. Toss with fennel seeds, lemon juice, and more red pepper flakes. Set aside.

recipe continues

4 pounds skinless,
   boneless chicken
   breast, cut into bite-size
   pieces

1 tablespoon olive oil

2 teaspoons minced garlic

1 teaspoon coarse sea salt

½ teaspoon crushed black
   pepper

¼ teaspoon dried thyme

1 red onion, chopped

1 cup sweet peppers, sliced

¾ cup dry white wine

Juice of ½ lemon

¼ cup pitted Castelvetrano
   olives

¼ cup kumquats

FOR THE COUSCOUS

1-pound box couscous,
   cooked

2 teaspoons olive oil

½ medium onion, minced

¼ teaspoon salt

2 tablespoons balsamic
   vinegar

2 teaspoons fresh flat-leaf
   parsley, chopped

PREPARE THE MEDITERRANEAN CHICKEN

5   Place diced chicken in a large bowl and coat with olive oil. Add garlic, sea salt, crushed black pepper, and thyme. Toss to coat.

6   Preheat a large skillet on medium-high heat. Add enough olive oil to coat the bottom of the pan, and sauté the red onion till lightly browned. Add the spiced chicken and sweet peppers, and continue to cook until the chicken is lightly browned and the onion and peppers are caramelized.

7   Deglaze with white wine and reduce to half (about 2 minutes). Add a squeeze of lemon juice, olives, and kumquats; cook for 3 minutes, or until thoroughly heated.

PREPARE THE COUSCOUS

8   Preheat a medium saucepan on medium-high and add the olive oil. Sauté the onion with salt until lightly browned. Reduce heat to medium and add the balsamic vinegar. Continue to sauté until the onion is caramelized and the vinegar is slightly reduced.

9   Remove from the heat. Toss with the cooked couscous and sprinkle in the parsley. Toss until evenly coated.

TO PLATE

10   Place a fair amount of couscous on the center of each plate. Top with the chicken and sauce. Place the eggplant alongside and slightly overlapping the couscous (for those partaking), and serve.

Approximate dose per serving is based on infusing 5 grams of cured/dried/decarbed cannabis into 5 ounces of oil.

SPICY MOROCCAN CANNA-LAMB TAGINE WITH CILANTRO & MINT

There is something incredibly comforting about this tagine. Maybe it's the fact that this hearty North African stew is chock-full of wonderful flavors, textures, and spices, or maybe it's the fact that it's lightly medicated. Either way, it's delicious and very calming. Serve with rice or alongside a heaping plate of Homemade Pita (page 220).

SERVINGS
8

PREP TIME
45
minutes

COOK TIME
3
hours and 20
minutes

APPROXIMATE
THC PER
SERVING*

10%: 7.6 mg

15%: 11.4 mg

20%: 15.2 mg

6 lamb shanks or 3 pounds lamb shoulder or lamb stew meat

2 tablespoons mint jelly

2 teaspoons kosher salt, plus more to taste

½ teaspoon cracked black pepper, plus more to taste

3 tablespoons extra-virgin olive oil

3 medium red onions, halved and sliced

4 cloves garlic, peeled and smashed

1-inch finger fresh turmeric, grated, or 1 teaspoon ground turmeric

½ teaspoon black cumin seeds

1   Cut lamb into bite-size pieces. In a medium bowl, toss the lamb with mint jelly, kosher salt, and pepper.

2   Heat the extra-virgin olive oil in a Dutch oven over medium-high heat. Sear the lamb in the hot oil until the lamb is golden brown on all sides, about 10 minutes. Lower the heat to medium; remove the lamb to a plate and set aside.

3   Carefully add the onions to the hot oil and season with salt and pepper. Sauté until the onions are slightly caramelized, about 10 minutes. Add the garlic, turmeric, cumin seeds, coriander, cilantro, red pepper flakes, and cinnamon stick to the onions, and sauté until fragrant, about 30 seconds.

½ teaspoon crushed
coriander

¼ cup cilantro, chopped
(reserve half for
garnish)

1 teaspoon red pepper
flakes

1 cinnamon stick

⅓ cup dark beer

1½ cups vegetable broth

½ cup dried apricots, cut
into small pieces

2 tablespoons canna-olive
oil

¼ cup chopped mint
leaves for garnish

4 Add beer and deglaze. Cook for about 5 minutes, until the beer is partially reduced. Add the vegetable broth and apricots and bring to a boil. Add the lamb back into the pot. Cover, and reduce the heat to low. Simmer, covered, for 3 hours, turning over once in the pot. Remove cover, add the canna-olive oil, and simmer for 5 more minutes, to allow the sauce to thicken slightly.

5 Garnish with cilantro and mint leaves, and serve.

* Approximate dose per serving is based on infusing 5 grams of cured/dried/decarbed cannabis into 5 ounces of oil.

RIB EYE WITH CANNA-BUTTERED BLACKENED CORN & CELTIC SEA SALT

I made this meal with Margaret Cho, one of my favorite comedians, and Kevin Pereira, host of the new series *Super Into* on truTV, and we had a blast. The magic is in the corn and is also drizzled onto the steak. This is a hearty meal that kicks in pretty quickly.

4 bone-in rib eye steaks, 1 inch thick

FOR THE RUB

2 teaspoons fresh tarragon, minced

2 teaspoons kosher salt

½ teaspoon ground ginger

½ teaspoon cayenne pepper

2 tablespoons coarsely ground pepper

FOR THE MARINADE

⅓ cup tamari soy sauce

½ cup olive oil

⅓ cup fresh pineapple juice

2 tablespoons dark cherry syrup or honey

¼ cup apple cider vinegar

2 teaspoons fresh garlic, minced

1   Mix together all the rub ingredients in a small bowl. Set aside.

2   In a separate bowl, mix together all the marinade ingredients. With your fingers, massage the rub into both sides of the steaks and refrigerate for 1 hour. Then place the steaks in a large ziplock bag and pour the marinade over them. Ensure that every part of each steak is coated. Refrigerate again for 1 hour.

3   Make sure the grill is clean. Season the grill by wiping it with a cloth dampened with vegetable oil, and allow it to heat up. Preheat to high. If you prefer to use an oven, set your broiler to 550°F.

4   Place the unshucked corn on the grill or under the broiler. Grill or broil for 24 minutes, turning the corn a quarter turn every 6 minutes. Remove the corn from the grill/broiler and set aside till cool enough to handle but still hot enough to melt butter.

5   While the corn is cooling, place steaks on the grill. For medium-rare steaks, place the steaks on the grill for 2 to 3 minutes, then rotate each steak 90° in the same spot on the grill for another 2 minutes (add another 1 or 2 minutes to each side if you're cooking at high altitude).

SERVINGS

4

PREP TIME

20

minutes

COOK TIME

25

minutes

IDLE TIME

2

hours

APPROXIMATE THC PER SERVING (DOES NOT INCLUDE THE FIVE-PEPPER BLAZED POTATOES)*

10%: 6.3 mg

15%: 9.5 mg

20%: 12.6 mg

FOR THE BLACKENED CORN

Vegetable oil for seasoning grill

4 ears of corn

1 tablespoon creamy canna-butter, plus 1 tablespoon grass-fed butter

Celtic Sea Salt

White pepper

Red chili flakes

TO FINISH

2 tablespoons olive oil

1 large red onion, sliced

1 pound cremini and/or portobello mushrooms, quartered

¼ cup white wine

1 teaspoon fresh destemmed tarragon leaves

2 teaspoons creamy canna-butter

Repeat the same process for the other side of the steak. Lower the grill temperature to medium and finish cooking for another 2 to 3 minutes on each side, either on the grill or in a cast-iron pan in a preheated (500ºF) oven.

6   While the steaks finish cooking, preheat a saucepan and add olive oil. Sauté the red onion until translucent, then add the mushrooms and continue to sauté until the onion is golden brown.

7   Deglaze with white wine, and reduce by half. Add the tarragon. Remove from heat and stir in the canna-butter. Set aside.

8   Do the "feel test" on your steaks (see sidebar, below). When they're done, remove them from the grill and season with a mist of fine sea salt. Let rest for 5 minutes.

9   Shuck the corn and use a sharp knife to slice the kernels off the ears into a large bowl. Add canna-butter mixture and toss until fully melted and corn is evenly coated. Sprinkle with Celtic Sea Salt, white pepper, and red chili flakes to taste. Finish with canna-mushrooms and onions.

10   Serve with Five-Pepper Blazed POTatoes (page 122).

BLACKENED CORN

APPROXIMATE THC PER SERVING*

10%:	2.5 mg
15%:	3.8 mg
20%:	5 mg

TO FINISH

APPROXIMATE THC PER SERVING*

10%:	3.8 mg
15%:	5.7 mg
20%:	7.6 mg

*Approximate dose per serving is based on infusing 5 grams of cured/dried/decarbed cannabis into 1⅓ sticks of butter.

STEAK FEEL TEST

This is a neat trick I learned from ourbestbites.com. The soft padded area on the palm of your hand under your thumb is a great grilling tool! Using your non-dominant hand, extend your fingers and use the pointer finger from your dominant hand to feel the padded area of your palm. It should feel soft and squishy. This is equivalent to the feel of a rare piece of meat. Next, bring the index finger and thumb of your non-dominant hand together and use both to feel the padded area again. It should feel a little firmer this time. This is equivalent to the feeling of a medium-rare piece of meat. And so on down the line until you get to the pinkie, which causes the padding of your palm to feel like a well-done piece of meat.

VEGETARIAN FIESTA NIGHT

Vegetable-Stuffed Enchiladas with Oaxacan Canna-Mole, Roasted Poblano & Potato Gratin and Kale Salad with Pumpkin Seeds & Cotija Cheese

Kudos to Chef Gillian Caballero Chase for teaching me how to make mole—cannabis-infused mole, to be exact. Chef Gillian, executive chef at the Nob Hill Grille in San Francisco, discovered that substituting coconut oil for lard instead of corn oil (which is the general substitute used in Mexico) will add some of the richness back into vegetarian versions of dishes that traditionally call for lard—and it has the benefit of being a lot healthier than either lard or corn oil. We hope you have a lot of fun with this collaboration. Invite some friends over and enjoy.

FULL MEAL

SERVINGS
8

PREP TIME
2
hours

COOK TIME
1
hour and 45
minutes

APPROXIMATE
THC PER
SERVING*

10%: 10.3 mg

15%: 15.6 mg

20%: 20.6 mg

Vegetable-Stuffed Enchiladas

SERVINGS
16

APPROXIMATE
THC PER
SERVING*

10%: 1.25 mg

15%: 1.9 mg

20%: 2.5 mg

* Approximate dose
per serving is based
on infusing 5 grams of
cured/dried/decarbed
cannabis into 5 ounces
of oil.

1 tablespoon olive oil

1 onion, minced

1 serrano chili, finely
diced

2 teaspoons Mexican
oregano

4 sprigs fresh thyme, or ½
teaspoon dried

1 red bell pepper

2 cups broccoli, chopped

¼ cup dry white wine

1½ teaspoons kosher salt

¼ teaspoon black pepper

16 corn tortillas

2 teaspoons canna-olive
oil, plus 2 teaspoons
extra-virgin or light
olive oil

Oaxacan Canna-Mole (see
286)

2 cups shredded jack
cheese

1   Preheat oven to 325°F.

2   Preheat a sauté pan and add the olive oil.
Add the onion and serrano chili and sauté on
high for 3 to 5 minutes, stirring often, until
lightly browned. Reduce heat to medium, and
add the oregano and thyme. Next, add the red
pepper, broccoli, wine, kosher salt, and black
pepper. Cook for another 3 to 4 minutes, just
until vegetables start to soften but still hold
their color. Remove from the heat.

3   To assemble the enchiladas, stack the
tortillas on a plate and cover with plastic wrap.
Microwave for 30 to 60 seconds, just to heat the
tortillas so that they are more pliable and won't
tear when rolled.

4   Brush each tortilla with a little of the
canna-olive oil.

5   Pour 1 cup of mole sauce into a baking dish
and spread evenly. Put another cup of sauce
into a separate dish, which will be used for
dipping the tortillas.

6   Take 1 tortilla, using tongs if too hot to
hold, and dip into the mole sauce. Be sure it is
coated, but shake off excess.

7   Put approximately 1 tablespoon of
vegetable mixture and 1 tablespoon of
shredded cheese in the middle of the tortilla,
then roll tightly. Place it in the baking dish,
then repeat with remaining tortillas, making
rows across.

8   Spoon another cup of mole sauce over
the enchiladas, and sprinkle with remaining
cheese. Bake for 20 minutes, uncovered.

Oaxacan Canna—Mole

SERVINGS
24

APPROXIMATE
THC PER
SERVING*

10%: 2.5 mg

15%: 3.7 mg

20%: 5 mg

Classic Oaxacan Mole is a dish often reserved for special meal preparations, such as at weddings or other family gatherings. It takes time to prepare, but it keeps very well, often developing more flavor as it sits for a week or more in the refrigerator. It also can be frozen and kept for several months. This recipe traditionally calls for lard and chicken stock, and it is very difficult to find a vegetarian version (this recipe purposefully will make more than what is needed for the enchiladas, so that you can store it for future use, or experiment using it with meat dishes). This mole can also be served over any roasted poultry or pork dish, and it is even delicious just with scrambled eggs and tortillas for a quick breakfast. You will be able to find the chilis, avocado leaves, canela, and chocolate at any Mexican grocery store—or you can order them online from gourmetsleuth.com if you don't have access to a Mexican grocery store.

5 pasilla chilies, dried

5 mulato chilies, dried

2 negro chilies, dried

2 chipotle chilies, dried

1 quart water

¼ cup light coconut oil

¼ pound tomatillos, peeled but left whole

½ pound tomatoes, cored but left whole

1 onion, halved

4 garlic cloves, peeled

¼ cup golden raisins

¼ cup almonds

¼ cup roasted peanuts

¼ cup pecans

1   Seed and devein all chilies by pulling off the stems and cracking them open. Shake out the seeds, saving them for step 3. (You might want to use gloves . . . and *do not* touch your nose, rub your eyes, or touch any other sensitive part of your body until you've washed your hands thoroughly. Trust me on this!)

2   Toast the chilies in an ungreased pan, being careful not to burn them. Soak in 1 quart of hot water for 30 minutes.

3   Meanwhile, in another small pan, fry the reserved chili seeds in 1 tablespoon of non-infused light coconut oil until blackened. Rinse in a strainer under hot water and set aside.

4   In the same ungreased pan, roast the tomatillos, tomatoes, onion, and garlic over medium heat until charred, turning frequently. Remove from the heat and set ingredients aside in a bowl.

¼ cup sesame seeds

¼ cup pumpkin seeds

¼ teaspoon black pepper

½ teaspoon cumin

½ teaspoon anise

3 whole cloves

3 whole allspice berries

½ teaspoon thyme

½ teaspoon oregano

1 slice challah, or sweet egg bread

1 quart vegetable stock

1 overripe banana, small

3 avocado leaves

2 whole cinnamon sticks (try to use real "Canela" from a Mexican grocery)

1 tablespoon kosher salt, plus more to taste

6 ounces Mexican chocolate

2 tablespoons canna-coconut oil, plus ⅓ cup coconut oil

Approximate dose per serving is based on infusing 5 grams of cured/dried/decarbed cannabis into 5 ounces of oil.

5   Using the same pan again, heat 1 tablespoon of non-infused coconut oil and add the raisins, nuts, seeds, black pepper, cumin, anise, cloves, allspice berries, thyme, and oregano, and let them begin to brown in the oil, about 2 minutes.

6   Immediately add another tablespoon of coconut oil, then fry the challah bread with the other items in the pan. Allow the bread to brown, turning frequently and adding more oil if necessary. Remove from heat and set ingredients aside in a bowl.

7   In a blender, mix the onion-tomato mixture until smooth, then set aside again. Do not rinse blender.

8   Using tongs, remove all the chilies from the water and place in the same blender. Reserve the soaking liquid. Blend the chilies and the reserved, blackened chili seeds with 1 cup soaking liquid and 1 cup vegetable stock until liquefied. Put the mixture through a strainer into a bowl and set aside.

9   Without cleaning the blender, blend the banana with the nut mixture and 2 cups of the vegetable stock. Set aside.

10   Heat 1 tablespoon of non-infused coconut oil in a large pan with a lid, and begin to "fry" the chili mixture, stirring slowly for 5 to 7 minutes, until the mixture darkens.

11   Using tongs, briefly heat the avocado leaves over an open flame to release their aroma, then add the leaves to the chili mixture.

12   Add the blended onion-tomato mixture to the sauce and cook for another 5 minutes. Add the banana-nut mixture, cinnamon sticks, and kosher salt. Slowly add more stock, as needed. (But don't thin it too much—the final step of adding the cannabis oil will aid in thinning the mixture.) Cover, and cook over low heat for 20 minutes to allow the sauce to thicken.

13   Break the chocolate pieces into the sauce and allow them to melt. Add more salt as needed for your taste. Re-cover and simmer for another 30 minutes. Turn off the heat, and allow the sauce to cool for 10 minutes. Remove the avocado leaves and cinnamon sticks. Place approximately 2 cups of sauce in a blender with the canna–coconut oil mixture and puree for 30 seconds, then add the blended mixture back into the rest of the sauce. Still off the heat and using a whisk, blend sauce very well for 2 minutes. If the sauce appears too thick to dip tortillas into, you can thin it with a little more vegetable stock.

Roasted Poblano & Potato Gratin

This is a variation of a classic French gratin dish. Since one can almost never use too much butter with potatoes, this recipe is easy to adjust for personal preferences of amounts of cannabis butter. However, due to the larger-than-normal amount of butter used, this recipe uses milk instead of heavy cream.

4 pounds Yukon Gold potatoes

1 tablespoon non-infused olive oil, for cooking

1 onion, diced

4 or 5 poblano chilies (peppers)

1½ cups whole milk

1½ cups to 2 cups shredded cheddar cheese

3 teaspoons salt

1 teaspoon white pepper

1 garlic clove

2 tablespoons canna-butter, plus ⅔ cup grass-fed butter

1   Preheat oven to 300°F.

2   Peel the potatoes and, using a mandoline, slice them very thin. Set aside in a bowl with cold water.

3   Heat the olive oil in a sauté pan and add the onion. Cook over high heat for 2 minutes to start the browning process, then lower heat to the lowest setting and leave onion to caramelize for 30 to 40 minutes.

4   Meanwhile, using tongs (or if you have one, a chili roaster), hold poblano chilies over open flame on stovetop, turning frequently, until skin is completely charred and black. Place charred chilies in a plastic bag and close securely. Allow to sit and steam in bag for 10 minutes. Then, carefully peel all skin from them. Slice chilies open and removed all seeds and veins. (You might want to use gloves.) Put 1 chili aside, and finely dice the remaining ones.

5   Place milk, the 1 non-diced chili, caramelized onion, salt, and white pepper in a blender. Liquefy.

6 Cut the garlic clove in half and, using the cut sides, rub it over the entire inside surface of the pot. Then take approximately 1 teaspoon of the canna-butter mixture and coat the entire inside of the pot.

7 Drain the potatoes. In a circular pattern, begin to arrange the potato slices in the pot to make one solid layer. Spoon and spread out a little bit of the diced chilies over this layer, then sprinkle with a handful of cheddar cheese. Continue in this manner, placing cheese and chilies on top of each layer of potato slices, with the exception of the final layer. Leave enough cheese to put on the top layer, but don't do it yet.

8 Place the pot on the stove over medium-high heat and pour in 1 cup of the milk-chili mixture. Swirl and shake the pot around so that the liquid spreads throughout all the potato layers. Bring to a boil, cover, lower heat to a simmer, and cook for 20 minutes. Remove lid.

9 Melt the remaining canna-butter and add to the remaining milk-chili mixture in the blender. Blend on high for 1 minute. Pour over the potato mixture, again swirling to ensure even coverage. Add the remaining cheddar cheese on top. Place in oven, uncovered, and bake for 60 to 90 minutes, until the top is brown and the potatoes are soft through.

Approximate dose per serving is based on infusing 5 grams of cured/dried/decarbed cannabis into 1⅓ sticks of butter.

Kale Salad with Pumpkin Seeds & Cotija Cheese

SERVINGS

8

APPROXIMATE
THC PER
SERVING*

10%:	3.8 mg
15%:	5.7 mg
20%:	7.6 mg

Kale is one of the only leafy greens that can actually benefit from sitting in the fridge with the dressing on. Other salad greens will wilt almost immediately, but kale can actually marinate and soften. This means it can also be dressed in advance and left to sit before being served, if you so choose. This salad is paired with other vegetables that will hold up well to marinating.

1 tablespoon non-infused olive oil, for cooking

1 shallot, finely diced

1½ bunches curly kale

1 garlic clove

1 teaspoon kosher salt

½ teaspoon honey

Juice of 4 limes

1 tablespoon white wine vinegar

½ teaspoon pepper

1 tablespoon canna–olive oil, plus 3 tablespoons extra-virgin olive oil

2 carrots, peeled and grated medium

1 red beet, peeled and grated medium

½ pint cherry tomatoes, each cut in half

1 cup toasted pumpkin seeds

1 cup crumbled Cotija cheese (or crumbled sheep's-milk feta if you cannot find Cotija)

1   Heat 1 tablespoon of cooking oil in small sauté pan and add shallot. Sauté over medium heat until golden brown, remove from heat, and set aside.

2   Wash kale and cut out the tougher end of the stems. With your hands, tear the kale into medium-large bite-size pieces. Place at bottom of large salad bowl.

3   Place garlic clove and salt in a mortar and pestle, and grind until they form a paste. Put the paste in a Mason jar and add the shallot, honey, lime juice, vinegar, pepper, and canna–olive oil mixture. Vigorously shake to emulsify the ingredients.

4   Add all the remaining vegetables and pumpkin seeds to the salad and toss well with the dressing. Adjust salt and pepper to taste. Top with crumbled cheese, and serve.

Approximate dose per serving is based on infusing 5 grams of cured/dried/decarbed cannabis into 5 ounces of oil.

METRIC CONVERSION CHART

Oven Temperature Equivalents

250°F = 120°C

275°F = 135°C

300°F = 150°C

325°F = 160°C

350°F = 180°C

375°F = 190°C

400°F = 200°C

425°F = 220°C

450°F = 230°C

475°F = 240°C

500°F = 260°C

Length Equivalents

¼ inch = 0.5 cm

½ inch = 1 cm

1 inch = 2.5 cm

6 inches = 15 cm

1 foot (12 inches) = 30 cm

Volume Equivalents

⅛ teaspoon = 0.5 ml

¼ teaspoon = 1 ml

½ teaspoon = ¹⁄₁₂ fluid ounce = 2 ml

1 teaspoon = ⅙ fluid ounce = 5 ml

1 tablespoon = 3 teaspoons = ½ fluid ounce = 15 ml

2 tablespoons = ⅛ cup = 1 fluid ounce = 30 ml

4 tablespoons = ¼ cup = 2 fluid ounces = 60 ml

5⅓ tablespoons = ⅓ cup = 3 fluid ounces = 80 ml

8 tablespoons = ½ cup = 4 fluid ounces = 120 ml

10⅔ tablespoons = ⅔ cup = 5 fluid ounces = 160 ml

12 tablespoons = ¾ cup = 6 fluid ounces = 180 ml

16 tablespoons = 1 cup = 8 fluid ounces = 240 ml

1 pint = 2 cups = 16 fluid ounces = 480 ml

1 quart = 4 cups = 32 fluid ounces = 960 ml

2 quarts = 8 cups = 64 fluid ounces = 1,920 ml

1 gallon = 4 quarts = 16 cups = 128 fluid ounces = 3,840 ml

Weight Equivalents

½ ounce = 15 g

1 ounce = 30 g

2 ounces = 55 g

4 ounces (¼ pound) = 115 g

5⅓ ounces (⅓ pound) = 150 g

8 ounces (½ pound) = 225 g

12 ounces (¾ pound) = 340 g

16 ounces (1 pound) = 455 g

24 ounces (1½ pounds) = 680 g

32 ounces (2 pounds) = 905 g

Acknowledgments

I AM INCREDIBLY GRATEFUL to God and the universe for all the signs and wonders that led me in this direction. I am particularly thankful for my three incredible sons, Matt, Jared, and Zach, for their constant and unconditional love and support and for allowing me the opportunity to show them that you can make any dream come true, no matter how crazy, as long as you're passionate, you believe in it, and you are dedicated to it. To my parents and brothers, for always being there for me, and specifically to my beautiful mother, for always encouraging me to experiment and create new recipes. I have cooked in kitchens all over the world and have yet to find one that is stocked with more appliances, tools, gadgets, and ingredients than my mother's.

A huge shout-out to my good friend and manager Brian Feit at BMF Media, who insisted that I write a cookbook because "it will help so many people," and who then introduced to me to HarperCollins. Together with his team, Brian has been leading me on this incredible journey. And to Justin Jones, the talented journalist at the *Daily Beast*, who took a chance and tried one of my first "tasteless" cupcakes. Justin, thanks for writing about it—and for introducing me to the world as the "Julia Child of weed."

To Brian Perrin for opening the door to HarperCollins, and to Karen Rinaldi, Senior Vice President and Executive Editor of HarperWave, for recognizing the importance of this cookbook and green-lighting the project. To Sarah Murphy, my wonderfully excited, patient, and understanding editor, for guiding me painlessly through the process of writing a cookbook for the first time. To Adrian Hale, a fantastic chef, an incredible artisan baker, and the best recipe tester I could have ever asked for. To Michael Burnham for his incredible macro shots of the cannabis featured in this book. And to the beautiful Leela Cyd, photographer par excellence, for her magnificent photos and flawless creative direction.

I also would like to thank the various chefs I have collaborated with and learned so much from over the past year: Chef J. P. Reyes, Google's vegan chef extraordinaire; the very talented and precise Chef Tadashi Miwa; and the beautiful Chef Gillian "La" Caballero. All three have recipes in this book. And to my sous-chef André Lujan, a talented chef at the L.A. Dodgers' Dugout Club, who has been by my side encouraging, testing, innovating, and helping me in so many ways.

To my friends Lilly, Shawn, Alex, Stanos, and Leo, who supported me every step of the way and who each had a hand in helping me get to where I am today. To Barry "Dovie" Friedman, for his encouragement to keep developing recipes, and for the use of his beautiful kitchen to create and test them.

To Weston Green, Tyler Gilden, and their teams at *Elite Daily*, for their awesome video that showed the world what I'm doing. To Andrew DeAngelo from Harborside Health Center, for his guidance early on and for allowing me, along with *Elite Daily*, to film my buying process at Harborside. To Chase and Sasha from Apothecarium SF, for opening my eyes to the future of edibles and the importance of understanding the different characteristics and effects of the various strains of cannabis.

To Emily Richardson and the rest of the folks at CW Analytical in Oakland, California, for all their help testing my butters, oils, and edibles. And to Dan Nascimbeni, for his hard work and patience in helping me develop the CBD/THC calculator.

This book is in your hands because of these incredible people, and I am eternally grateful to all of them—and to you.

About the Author

Dubbed the "Julia Child of weed" by the *Daily Beast*, the "Ganja Gourmet" by *Newsweek*, and the "King of Edibles" by *Elite Daily*, JeffThe420Chef has been cooking with cannabis since 2007. At first, it was just for a few friends with medical marijuana prescriptions and recreationally for friends in states that legalized. Early on, Jeff realized that high-CBD strains of cannabis are the ones that help MMJ patients the most. He began researching CBD-rich strains and creating specially cured canna-butters and canna-oils to incorporate these into his gourmet recipes. Each butter and oil is made from a specific CBD-rich strain of cannabis or a combination of THC- and CBD-rich strains known to help treat specific conditions.

Jeff's gourmet "medibles" and "medible meals" were a hit. Yet from the beginning there was always the issue of "that cannabis taste." In 2014, Jeff invented an intricate process that effectively neutralizes the cannabis taste in his butters and oils when cooked—and, as they say, the rest is history. Today, JeffThe420Chef is known for his powerful "tasteless" and "light-tasting" canna-butters and canna-oils and for his incredible medible meals and desserts, and now you can make them, too. Voilà!

Contributors

Leela Cyd

Leela Cyd is a food, travel, and lifestyle photographer based in Santa Barbara, California. Her work has appeared in many cookbooks, commercial projects, and magazines such as *Sweet Paul*, *Food & Wine*, *Cooking Light*, and *Kinfolk*. Leela is a storyteller first and foremost and can often be found shooting artists, makers, grandmothers, cooks, and foragers around the world and sharing inspiration on her eponymous blog.

Chef Adrian Hale

Adrian J. S. Hale has been writing professionally for over a decade. She has worked for various food and lifestyle publications, including filling in as assistant food editor at *Country Living* and working on the editorial research team at *Saveur*.

In 2004, she started writing a regular food column for the *Orlando Weekly*, where she developed food-related stories and wrote restaurant critiques. For the past eight years, she has been freelancing as a recipe developer and writing stories for publications such as *Saveur*, *Culture*, *Mix*, and others. She is the editor of the online magazine *Communal Table*, which shares articles and recipes quarterly. She is also the food blogger and baker extraordinaire behind thousandbitesofbread.com.

She and her family travel extensively, but they settle much of the time in Portland, Oregon. You will most likely find Adrian elbow-deep in red fife flour and shaping loaves of *levain*. She pauses to hike, forage, delve into a good book, or sit around a table with the people she loves.

Chef Tadashi Miwa

Half Filipino and half Japanese, Chef Tadashi was born and raised in the beautiful Philippine Islands. He has traveled the world extensively, and his culture and travels have hugely inspired his passion for cooking. Based in San Francisco, Tadashi received his chef training from the Culinary Institute of America at Greystone in the Napa Valley. After culinary school, he worked for the highly acclaimed Michelin-rated One Market restaurant in San Francisco's financial district. He now works as a chef for a well-known luxury resort brand. Chef Tadashi regards the Bay Area as a culinary mecca with an abundance of resources available all year long. His culinary ideal is cooking with ingredients that are seasonal, locally sourced, sustainable, and organic. Tadashi loves seafood and sushi, in particular. Being a big foodie, he either cooks at home or visits his favorite sushi place on his days off. Tadashi's style is fresh, clean, and uncomplicated, highlighting the real flavors and textures of ingredients that go well together. He dreams of having his own little place on the beach in Asia, where people will gather to celebrate, and where he can make the ocean his garden and use its bounty to bring his flavor creations to life.

Chef Gillian "La" Caballero

Chef "La" Caballero began cooking at the age of eight, inspired by the combination of her father's vast cookbook collection and her stepmother's (self-admitted) complete lack of any cooking skills. Taking matters into her own hands and teaching herself to read and follow recipes, she became the self-taught chef of the family well before turning ten years old. Having grown up in California and having worked in Bay Area restaurants for more than twenty years, she has developed a personal style of cooking that firmly follows the philosophy of using seasonal, high-quality ingredients and avoiding all processed foods and chemical additives. For the ten years prior to finally officially attending culinary school, she began to cook exclusively vegetarian, vegan, and raw cuisine. Also, having lived and extensively traveled in Mexico and Italy (where her ancestors are from), she has focused her cooking style to reflect the classic recipes of those areas, but with healthier lifestyle modifications and a California perspective.

Chef "La" Caballero lost her father to cancer in 2008. At that time she began to contemplate the medical benefits of cooking savory, non-blood-sugar-spiking, whole-food-based foods with cannabis, at the same time as she was attending the City College of San Francisco's prestigious Culinary Arts and Hospitality Program. She is currently working as a chef in San Francisco, while simultaneously founding her new company, Green Light Naturals, which will provide a combination of raw and cooked food-based wholesome products for the medical cannabis community.

Chef J. P. Reyes

In 2013, J. P. left his job in human resources to venture out into the wilds of the culinary world. With no income, he figured the best way to learn is in a real kitchen. The morning he quit his job, J. P. literally walked around San Francisco, popping into different restaurants to ask if he could "stage" (intern) for them. Out of all the restaurants he asked, Cotogna said yes! That was J. P.'s first real experience in a professional kitchen; J. P. got through the day, but it was tough. There was an etiquette he didn't know, a lingo he didn't understand, and a technique that was beyond him. Luckily, Cotogna was patient with him, and it took only that one day to validate for him that this was what he wanted to dedicate his life to.

Since then, J. P. has been on a crash course through life's kitchen. He landed his first *real* gig staging at Spice Kit. J. P. worked his way up to line cook and in just a few months was offered the opportunity to open and manage its second location. In that same year, he worked at Drake as the executive chef, helping it develop its first happy hour and brunch programs. J. P. then tried his luck at his own food business, but just as things were picking up, he was offered a job at Google San Francisco! J. P. is currently at Google and recently transitioned from lead vegan chef to sous-chef. In his free time J. P. experiments with pop-up dining events, to explore the world of comfort food and develop dishes that satisfy both vegans and omnivores.

Michael Burnham

Michael Burnham's passion for photography was sparked when, at the age of nine, he began borrowing an old camera of his father's, eventually receiving his own as a gift. With his passion discovered and his fate sealed, he actively improved his skills and knowledge of the medium throughout his teenage years. After high school he moved to California, where he received a bachelor of fine arts degree in art photography from CSU Long Beach, the largest campus in the California State University system. Michael has nineteen years of experience as a professional photographer, with experience in the fields of product photography, architecture, modeling and fashion, events, portraiture, and fine art.

Resources

Badiner, Alan. "High on Health: Cannabinoids in the Food Supply," *Waking Times*, April 25, 2013, http://www.wakingtimes.com/2013/04/25/high-on-health-cbd-in-the-food-supply/.

Bittman, Mark. "Cooking at High Altitudes." In *How to Cook Everything*. New York: Houghton Mifflin Harcourt, 2008.

Burnett, Malik. "Medical Marijuana: Much More Than Just THC and CBD." Medical Jane, accessed November 19, 2015, http://www.medicaljane.com/2014/05/14/thc-cbd-and-more-the-entourage-effect-of-whole-plant-cannabis-medicine/.

Canani, Roberto Berni, et al. "Potential Beneficial Effects of Butyrate in Intestinal and Extraintestinal Diseases." *World Journal of Gastroenterology* 17, no. 12 (March 28, 2011): 1519–28, accessed November 19, 2015, http://www.ncbi.nlm.nih.gov/pmc/articles/PMC3070119/.

"Cannabinoid Chemical Details." Steep Hill Labs, accessed November 17, 2015, http://www.steephilllab.com/resources/cannabinoid-and-terpenoid-reference-guide.

"Cannabis Dosing." Project CBD, accessed November 23, 2015, https://www.projectcbd.org/cannabis-dosing.

"The Cannabis Rescheduling Petition." Drug Science, accessed November 17, 2015, http://www.drugscience.org/Petition/C2E.html.

Coleman, Michael D. *Human Drug Metabolism: An Introduction*. 2nd edition. Oxford, UK: John Wiley and Sons, 2010.

"Endocannabinoid System." Wikipedia, last modified December 21, 2015, https://en.wikipedia.org/wiki/Endocannabinoid_system.

"Factors Influencing Psychopharmacological Effect," Drug Library, accessed November 18, 2015, http://druglibrary.eu/library/reports/nc/nc1d.htm.

"5 Must-Know Facts About Cannabinol (CBD)." Leaf Science, accessed November 17, 2015, http://www.leafscience.com/2014/02/23/5-must-know-facts-cannabidiol-cbd/.

"Getting Familiar with THCA." Cornerstone, accessed November 11, 2015, http://cornerstonecollective.com/getting-familiar-with-thca/.

Gunnars, Kris. "Why Grass-Fed Butter Is Good for You." *Authority Nutrition*, November 2013, http://authoritynutrition.com/grass-fed-butter-superfood-for-the-heart/.

"Harle-Tsu." Verdabase, accessed November 23, 2015, http://verdabase.com/strains/4d3936ee-6a70-3d79-9f37-55d376c75912.

Heustis, Marilyn A. "Human Cannabinoid Pharmacokinetics." *Chemistry and Biodiversity* 4, no. 8 (August 2007): 1770–1804, accessed November 24, 2015, http://www.ncbi.nlm.nih.gov/pmc/articles/PMC2689518/.

"How To: Grill the Perfect Steak." Our Best Bites, accessed September 4, 2015, http://ourbestbites.com/2011/08/how-to-grill-the-perfect-steak/.

Hudak, Marissa, et al. "Edible Cannabis-Induced Psychosis: Intoxication and Beyond." *American Journal of Psychiatry* 172, no. 9 (September 1, 2015): 911–12), accessed November 19, 2015, http://ajp.psychiatryonline.org/doi/abs/10.1176/appi.ajp.2015.15030358?journalCode=ajp.

J, Sirius. "The Anatomy of a Trichome. *High Times*, March 27, 2015, http://www.hightimes.com/read/anatomy-trichome.

———. "What Is the Real Boiling Point of THC?" *High Times*, July 10, 2015, http://www.hightimes.com/read/what-real-boiling-point-thc.

Lee, Martin A. "CBD Misconceptions." Project CBD, accessed November 23, 2015, https://www.projectcbd.org/article/cbd-misconceptions.

———. "Talking Terpenes." *High Times*, April 8, 2013, http://www.hightimes.com/read/talking-terpenes.

New Frontier. *Cannabis Science: How Marijuana Affects Health*, 2013, http://topdocumentaryfilms.com/cannabis-science-how-marijuana-affects-health/.

Rahn, Bailey. "Sativa, Indica, and Hybrid: What's the Difference Between Cannabis Types?" Leafly, accessed November 13, 2015, https://www.leafly.com/news/cannabis-101/sativa-indica-and-hybrid-whats-the-difference-between-cannabis-ty.

Russo, Ethan B. "Taming THC: Potential Cannabis Synergy and Phytocannabinoid-Terpenoid Entourage Effects." *British Journal of Pharmacology* 163, no. 7 (August 2011): 1344–64, accessed November 19, 2015, https://ncbi.nlm.nih.gov/pmc/articles/PMC3165946.

Sharma, Priyamvada, et al. "Chemistry, Metabolism, and Toxicology of Cannabis: Clinical Implications." *Iranian Journal of Psychiatry* 7, no. 4 (Fall 2012): 149–56, accessed November 25, 2015, http://www.ncbi.nlm.nih.gov/pmc/articles/PMC3570572/.

"Unprecedented Healing Power." Patients for Medical Cannabis, accessed November 19, 2015, https://patients4medicalmarijuana.wordpress.com/2013/04/26/cbd-unprecedented-healing-power/.

"What Is Miracle Fruit." Miracle Fruit USA, accessed September 23, 2015, http://www.miraclefruitusa.com/.

Index